Silver Wire Jewelry

Projects to Coil, Braid & Knit

Irene From Petersen

Silver Wire Jewelry

Projects to Coil, Braid & Knit

LARK BOOKS

A Division of
Sterling Publishing Co., Inc.
New York

Library of Congress Cataloging-in-Publication Data

Peterson, Irene From.
  [Sxlvmykker i spiral. Eng]
  Silver wire jewelry : projects to coil, braid & knit / Irene From Peterson; photographs by Niels Jensen.
  p. cm.
  Includes index.
  ISBN 1-57990-645-1 (hardcover)
  1. Jewelry making. 2. Wire craft. 3. Silver jewelry. I. Title.
  TT212.P4816 2005
  745.594'2--dc22

                                    2004014705

  10 9 8 7 6

English Translation © Lark Books 2004
Originally published as Sølvsmykker i spiral, strik og flet by Irene From Petersen
© 2001 Aschehoug Dansk Forlag A/S

Published by Lark Books, A Division of Sterling Publishing Co., Inc.
387 Park Avenue South, New York, N.Y. 10016

Distributed in Canada by Sterling Publishing,
c/o Canadian Manda Group, 165 Dufferin St., Toronto, Ontario, Canada M6K 3H6

Distributed in the United Kingdom by GMC Distribution Services,
Castle Place, 166 High Street, Lewes, East Sussex, England BN7 1XU

Distributed in Australia by Capricorn Link (Australia) Pty Ltd.,
P.O. Box 704, Windsor, NSW 2756 Australia

Photographs by Niels Jensen

Cover design: Anne Houe

Drawings by Birgitte Ahlmann

Type and repro: NordGraf,
Copenhagen

Printed by Sandill Grafisk
Produktion

Binding: D.L. Clements Eftf

Layout and dtp: Torben E.
Mortensen

Typeface: Minion

Editing: Kirsten Corvinius &
Torben E. Mortensen

English Version

Editor:
Suzanne J. E. Tourtillott

Production: Dana Irwin

Technical Consultant:
Joanna Gollberg

Translation: Robin Hansen

Every effort has been made to ensure that all the information in this book is accurate. However, due to differing conditions, tools, and individual skills, the publisher cannot be responsible for any injuries, losses, and other damages that may result from the use of the information in this book.

If you have questions or comments about this book, please contact:
Lark Books, 67 Broadway, Asheville, NC 28801 (828) 253-0467

Manufactured in China

ISBN 13: 978-1-57990-645-0
ISBN 10: 1-57990-645-1

For information about custom editions, special sales, premium and corporate purchases, please contact Sterling Special Sales Department at 800-805-5489 or specialsales@sterlingpub.com.

CONTENTS

FOREWORD

I'm continually fascinated by the different forms of artistic jewelry available to students on a variety of TV shows and websites and in magazines and books. However, I find it remarkable how similar both the jewelry and the choice of jewelry materials are from country to country—no matter how far apart they may be in physical distance or in culture and tradition.

Jewelry fashion seems to be more or less the same throughout the world. This, I feel, limits the possibilities available to us. Wearing unique jewelry, specially designed, in colors and materials flattering to the wearer, is a great pleasure—not least for the designer.

Historically, there are many examples of completely simple, handsome, and aesthetic jewelry forms, and they continue to be used today.

Nowadays, the simplicity of these original forms is sometimes overburdened with things and effects, drowned in the ornate. But whether you prefer the simple or the highly decorative, much can be accomplished with just beads and silver. Beads have long been admired and valued, both for ornamentation and as trade goods, from the distant past to the present. The same is true of silver, which is used in jewelry production in both its natural and colored versions.

New materials, including colored wires and steel wire, are emerging that can be used with the more familiar materials.

When designing your own jewelry, keep in mind that within each piece, elements must combine to produce integrity in shape, color, and materials. One element given particular attention in this book is the coil, with its characteristic and exciting form and possibilities. The coil is infinite—as is its design potential within the lexicon of jewelry design. You have only to begin.

Take pleasure in your work and have fun.

IRENE FROM PETERSEN

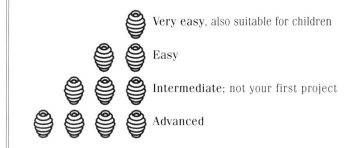

Skill Levels

Every project is rated according to its difficulty. In addition, the book is arranged so that the techniques described in one section are used and further developed in the next. It would thus be to your advantage to start with the first section if you making jewelry for the first time.

Very easy, also suitable for children

Easy

Intermediate; not your first project

Advanced

MATERIALS

In each section, I indicate which metals are best suited to the technique being shown. It's very important to use only metals designed for jewelry production, because it's not worth risking nickel allergy. Many types of acceptable wire are available for a reasonable price. If you must use a substitute for the wire used in the project, it's preferable to use the alternatives recommended in each section.

Copper. A pure metal that is available in gauges starting at .5 mm. Copper wires are soft and easy to work with. Many people who wear copper jewelry find that it marks their skin, so it's best to combine it with other metals so that the copper pieces don't directly touch your skin.

Colored Copper Wire. Available in various colors, this wire has a coating that in certain circumstances may peel off. However, it's very soft and easy to work with. Colored wire is available in gauges starting at .3 mm, in different qualities and at varying prices.

Silver-Plated Wire. This is usually copper wire with an ultrathin coating of silver. The wire is somewhat stiff to work with and isn't good for knitting, but it can be used for both braiding and twisting. This wire may be more difficult to find, but some retailers make it available in various gauges, starting at .4 mm.

Gold-Filled Wire. As the name implies, gold-filled wire looks like pure gold but is actually silver wire coated with a thin layer of gold. The wire comes in gauges from .3 mm; the quality and prices available will vary.

Tiger Tail. An unbelievably strong wire you can't tear apart, consisting of twisted wire covered with plastic. It comes in many colors and gauges. Tiger tail has a mind of its own, and it doesn't take much for it to snap or kink up. These problems can't be fixed, but if you're fond of using it, you learn to live with them.

Silver Wire. Silver is rated by its purity, with numbers indicating the percentage of pure silver in the alloy and its hardness, whether the wire is dead soft, half-soft, or hard to work with. Only soft wire is used in this book.

.999 Silver. This type is made of $^{999}/_{1000}$ pure silver and is also called "fine silver." Fine silver is available only as soft wire and is *very* soft and easy to work with. This is the best wire to use for braiding and knitting. And since it's only sold in spools, total lengths aren't given in the project instructions.

.925 Silver. Sterling silver is 92.5 percent pure silver and 7.5 percent copper. It's available in gauges from .4 mm.

Clasps and end pieces are available in many variations, qualities, and prices. Remember that it's often the finishing that adds that little extra touch to make a piece truly pleasing.

Crimp beads are used to lock beads or stones onto the wire. They are placed on the wire and clamped on with setting pliers or chain-nose pliers. Crimp beads come in various sizes and in brass, gold, gold-filled, and sterling silver.

TOOLS

It doesn't take many tools—or expensive ones—to create your own jewelry. Often you can substitute something you already have for some of the more expensive specialty tools. Who would guess, for example, that a pasta maker could be used for something other than making noodles? It's quite possible to use it to harden metal and to produce certain special effects.

In each section, you'll find a list of the tools needed for the techniques.

A basic kit of jeweler's tools includes:

Narrow Chain-Nose Pliers. Two pairs are used for joining rings made from conventional round wire.

Wide Flat-Nose Pliers. Two pairs are used for joining rings made from heavy or half-round wire.

Curved Needle-Nose Pliers. These are used to pinch in close quarters where normal needle-nose pliers may not be able to get in; used to make loops and eyes.

Wire Cutters. Used to cut wire.

Small Vise. The vise clamps wire or holds a drill.

Eggbeater Drill. Used to turn coils. A simple hand drill is recommended over an electric drill, because the hand drill stops turning the instant you stop turning the handle, but an electric drill will always make a few more turns before stopping, possibly causing injury.

Coiling Tool. A new device has come on the market that helps you make coils. It does the same job as the hand drill and can hold many different sizes of mandrels and wires. You can hold the device in your hand while turning the coils, which makes it easy for children to use.

Ring Mandrel. A long, slender cone used to form and size finger rings. A small wooden cone can be used if you're working only with fine wire.

Bracelet Mandrel. A long, fat, round or oval cone used to shape and size bracelets, available in steel and wood. A pipe or similarly shaped object can be substituted.

Plastic Hammer. When shaping metal by hammering it, use a plastic hammer to prevent metal from becoming brittle and breaking. Cover the jewelry with a piece of leather to protect the metal from hammer marks.

Piece of Soft Leather. Leather protects the metal from tool marks, but you can also use it to shield your fingers from the metal and the tools you're using.

Jeweler's Saw and Blades. A special metal saw used if you're making your own rings. Always use the thinnest possible blade, and insert the blade so that the sawteeth point down like the branches on a Christmas tree. Tighten the blade until it makes a fine high note when plucked, and always saw with gentle vertical strokes.

Pasta Maker. Use the pasta maker only after careful planning, since metal on metal results in hardening of one of them, and the wire may become brittle or even break. For a special effect in a piece, one or two strands can be flattened by pulling them through the pasta maker, contrasting a handsome flat surface with all the round strands. Wire and long S-clasps can be hardened and strengthened by running them through the machine several times.

Rotary Tumbler. Polish your jewelry to make it look professional. For some techniques the tumbler is necessary to make the wire ends smooth, though you can file the ends of the figure eights before closing them if you don't have a tumbler. If it's made of metal, the outside of the tumbler's drum can be used as a mandrel for forming neck rings.

The drum should contain about 2.2 pounds (1 kg) of polishing medium (usually stainless steel balls), a little burnishing compound, and water to cover the contents. Jewelry should be polished for 20 to 60 minutes. Empty the contents into a sieve.

Block of Wood. A piece of hardwood, drilled with $\frac{7}{8}$- to $3\frac{1}{4}$-inch (2 to 8 mm) holes. A braided piece can be pulled through a hole to even it up and smooth its surface.

Soft Brass-Bristled Brush. Use as an alternative to tumble-polishing, although it doesn't give as fine a polish as the rotary tumbler.

Metal Files. Used to smooth wire ends. You'll need small files in an assortment of shapes.

Mandrels. Long metal rods in assorted diameters. Some projects require mandrels up to 20 inches (50 cm) long. In other cases, you can use a knitting needle with the end sawn off.

Skewer. Use as a mandrel to make fine coils.

Knitting Needle. 3.5 mm, for knitting projects.

Crochet Hook. 2.5 mm, for crocheted projects.

HARDENING THE WIRE

When making finger rings, it's beneficial to harden the wire by hammering it lightly while the ring is on a mandrel. The ring will then keep its shape better. (See also the comments in the section on the pasta maker, page 9.)

GLUING

If the end pieces can't be attached any other way, you'll have to glue them with a two-part epoxy. Shape the jewelry ends into the end pieces before mixing the glue. A tight fit will give the glue a better bond.

Mix the glue according to directions on the container. Dip the ends of the jewelry into the glue and push the end pieces on. Immediately wipe off any excess glue. Allow the glue to harden completely, up to 24 hours, before attaching rings or a clasp. If the jewelry is to be oxidized, do that before any gluing.

OXIDIZING

The easiest way to color metal is to use liver of sulfur, which can be purchased in any drugstore. Liver of sulfur is yellow and sold in liquid or in a lump form that must be dissolved in water. Dissolve a ¼-ounce (7-g) lump of liver of sulfur in 1.6 quarts (1.5 L) of warm water in a glass jar with a lid. Adding a little ammonium bicarbonate will increase the shelf life of the solution, but it won't alter the resulting color of the metal.

First, wash the jewelry with dish detergent. Holding the jewelry with a wire, so that your skin won't come in contact with the liver of sulfur solution, submerse the piece and close the cover quickly, as it smells awful. When the piece is the right color, lift it out and rinse it thoroughly in running water. Rubbing exposed surfaces with powdered pumice brings out the color. Many effects can be achieved with oxidizing and polishing. Oxidized jewelry can be safely tumble-polished.

Jewelry made from copper, silver, and silver plate can be oxidized.

MAINTENANCE

In use, jewelry occasionally needs to be cleaned or freshened up. If the piece has freshwater pearls, a soft brass-bristled brush can be used on the metal only, but never on the pearls. The tumbler is the best way to clean silver or copper jewelry, and silver plate is best cleaned in a flatware cleaning solution. Using a cleaning solution is also an alternative if no tumbler is available, but don't use it on oxidized jewelry or the dark color will disappear.

Notes About Suppliers

Usually, the supplies you need for making the projects in Lark books can be found at your local craft supply store or retail business relevant to the topic of the book. Occasionally, however, you may need to buy materials or tools from specialty suppliers. In order to provide you with the most up-to-date information, we have created a listing of suppliers on our Web site, which we update on a regular basis. Visit us at www.larkbooks.com, click on "Craft Supply Sources," and then click on the relevant topic. You will find numerous companies listed with their web address and/or mailing address and phone number.

Making jewelry from wire coils, or connected spirals, is not a recent invention. Jewelers all over the world have always been fascinated by the simple, mystical, and infinite shape of the spiral. Let yourself become caught up in the world of spirals and inspired by their myriad possibilities. In this section, I'll show you how to use coils in jewelry, alone or in combination with other elements.

Materials and Tools for the Projects

You'll need a vise, an eggbeater drill, winding mandrels of various sizes, two pairs of chain-nose pliers, a piece of soft leather, a hook that will fit your drill chuck, a small file, wire cutters, round-nose pliers, two pairs of flat-nose pliers, curved needle-nose pliers, a bracelet mandrel, a ring mandrel, a rotary tumbler, a plastic hammer, a jeweler's saw and blades, and a long ruler or tape measure.

Use round and half-round sterling silver wire, or any metal wire intended for jewelry. In any of these projects, a less expensive wire of the same gauge can be substituted.

MAKING COILS

Fasten the vise to a table and clamp the hand drill in it, as shown at right. Firmly

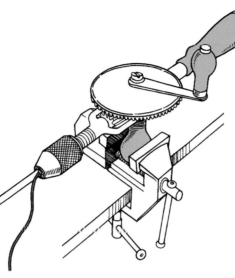

fasten a mandrel in the chuck. If you're using a very long mandrel, it's helpful to support the far tip to keep it from moving around.

Put the wire into the chuck next to the mandrel. Pull down on the wire and begin

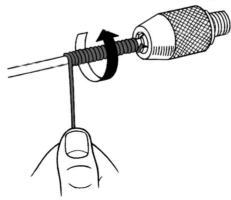

to turn the drill slowly, as shown below. As you near the end, again go slowly so that the wire won't hurt you if it whips out of your fingers.

Finish the Coil

Work one side of a flat-nose plier in under the first circle of the coil. Flip it up.

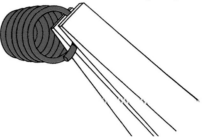

Grasp the remaining coils with your fingers while with the pliers you bend the

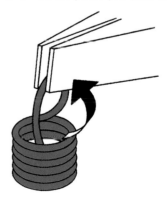

circle up in the middle, perpendicular to the rest of the coil and centered over it.

COIL NECKLACE WITH SILVER TUBE

  Length: 14 inches (35 cm)
without clasp

MATERIALS AND TOOLS

3-mm mandrel

*13 ¼ feet (4 m) of sterling silver wire,
18 gauge (1 mm)*

*80 rings made from 20-gauge (.8 mm)
sterling silver wire on a 2.8-mm mandrel*

Sterling silver lobster claw clasp, 12 mm

*12-inch (30 cm) section of curved sterling
silver tube with an inside diameter of
5 mm, available from specialty jewelry
suppliers*

Photo on page 14

Create the coil.

Measure off the correct length and twist-
lift the last ring on both ends of the coil.

Assemble two chain segments, 1-¼ inch
(3 cm) and 2-¾ inches (7 cm) long, pairing the rings two by two. See page 31 for
how to join rings.

Attach the clasp to one end. Slide the silver tube onto the chain.

CHAIN BRACELET WITH COIL

  Length: 6 ½ inches (16 cm)
without clasp

MATERIALS AND TOOLS

3-mm mandrel

*24 ⅜ inches (61 cm) of sterling silver wire,
18 gauge (1 mm)*

*23 rings made from 14-gauge (1.5 mm)
sterling silver wire on a 5-mm mandrel*

Sterling silver lobster claw clasp, 11 mm

Photo on page 14

Make the coil.

Lift the outermost circles and twist
them perpendicular to the coil, centered
over it.

Assemble the chain by joining the rings
one on one. See page 31 for how to join
rings. Attach it to one end of the coil. The
clasp is attached to the free end of the
chain and catches directly onto the coil.

COIL BEADS

First make the slender coil.

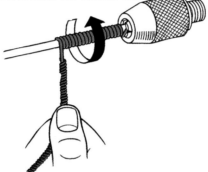

Thread the slender coil onto the heavier
wire and wind the heavy wire around the
mandrel, as shown.

Wind the heavy wire around the mandrel
until you reach the point where you want
the slender coil to start. Push the coil up
to the mandrel. Help the thin coil and the
heavy wire around the mandrel for the
first couple of turns. When the slender
spiral is used up, continue turning with
only the heavier wire. If the slender coil
segment is to be shaped onto the heavier
coil, do so while the heavy coil is still on
the mandrel.

Shape the bead further by twisting it in a
piece of soft leather while it's still on the
mandrel, as shown, optionally making it a

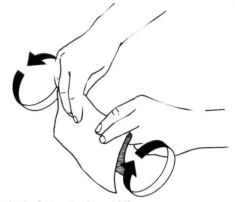

little fatter in the middle.

With flat-nose pliers, tuck the ends of

 the bead into
it slightly, as
shown below,
so that no
sharp ends
are sticking out.

NECKLACE WITH COIL BEAD

  Length: 15 ⅝ inches
(39 cm) without clasp

MATERIALS AND TOOLS

Coil Bead

2.5-mm mandrel

*4 ¼ feet (1.3 m) of sterling silver wire,
18 gauge (1 mm)*

Necklace

5-mm mandrel, 20 inches (50 cm) long

*10 feet (3 m) of half-round sterling
silver wire, 2 x 1 mm*

Sterling silver spring ring clasp, 15 mm

Photo on page 15

Make the slender coil. Slide the coil bead
7 ⅝ inches (19 cm) in onto the twisting
of the heavy coil. Lift and twist the outermost circles of the heavy coil perpendicular to the coil. Put on the spring ring
clasp. Oxidize and polish.

PLYING WIRES

Plying—twisting two strands together—makes the finished piece a little more special. Use this technique in places that seem to need a little extra punch.

Wire 22 to 16 gauge (.6 mm to 1.2 mm) is best suited for plying.

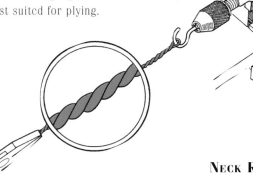

Mount a hook into the drill chuck.

Find the center of the wire and bend it onto the hook. Hold the wire as taut as possible with a pair of flat-nose pliers while turning the drill. In this case, the job will be much easier with two people, one to hold the pliers, the other to turn the drill.

Twist until you think the twist is tight enough (careful: the wire can break).

NECK RING WITH PLIED COIL BEAD

Length: 15¼ inches (38 cm) without clasp

MATERIALS AND TOOLS

Coil Bead

2.5-mm mandrel

6⅝ feet (2 m) of sterling silver wire, 22 gauge (.6 mm)

Heavy Coil

3.5-mm mandrel, 20 inches (50 cm) long

7 feet (2.1 m) of half-round sterling silver wire, 2 x 1 mm

Supporting Inside Wire

16 inches (40 cm) of copper or sterling silver wire, 8 gauge (3 mm)

Photo on page 15

Ply the doubled 22-gauge (.6 mm) wire to 36 inches (90 cm). From this plied wire, make the slender coil on the 2.5-mm mandrel.

Form the heavy coil on the 3.5-mm mandrel, and twist the plied coil bead 6-⅞ inches (17 cm) into the heavy coil.

Form the necklace from the 8-gauge (3 mm) wire around something the right size to fit the neck. Smooth the ends by filing them so that they won't scratch. Bend the ends inward a little when the necklace is the right shape. Harden the wire.

Twist the coil onto the necklace. Pinch the ends of the heavy coil closed so that the heavy wire can't be pushed out.

Oxidize and polish.

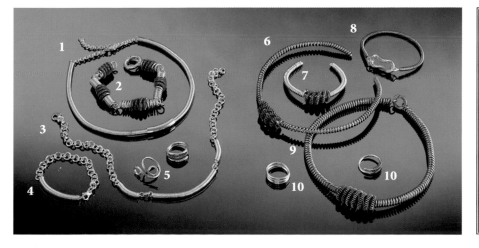

SILVER BRACELET WITH COIL BEAD

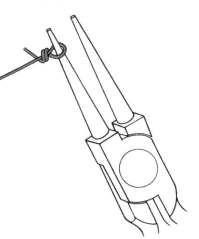

28- to 20-gauge (.3 to 0.8 mm) wire

🐝🐝🐝 Length: 6 ⅞ inches (17 cm)

MATERIALS AND TOOLS

Coil Bead

2.5-mm mandrel

4 ⅛ feet (1.25 m) of sterling silver wire, 18 gauge (1 mm)

Heavy Coil

3.5-mm mandrel

3 ⅓ feet (1 m) of half-round sterling silver wire, 2 x 1 mm

Supporting Inside Wire

6 ⅞ inches (17 cm) of copper or sterling silver wire, 8 gauge (3 mm)

Photo on page 15

Make and oxidize the slender coil for the bead.

Start the coil bead 2 ¾ inches (7 cm) into the heavy coil.

Shape the 8-gauge (3 mm) wire on a bracelet mandrel. Round the ends with a file to keep them from scratching. Harden the wire.

Turn the heavy coil, with bead, onto the 8-gauge (3 mm) wire. Pinch the ends closed so that the supporting wire can't be pushed out.

Finally, polish the piece.

MAKING END EYES

Here are two good techniques when you need an eye at the end of a wire; both work well.

Hold on to the round-nose pliers while twisting the short end of the wire.

Snip off the extra and pinch the end in close with curved needle-nose pliers.

18- to 16-gauge (1 to 1.2 mm) wire

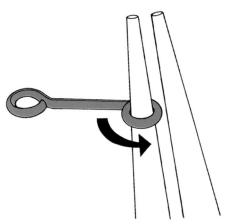

A short way down the round-nose pliers, twist the wire into an eye. Grasp the wire with the pliers at the base of the eye. Turn it slightly in the opposite direction to center the finished eye on the end of the wire.

NECKLACE WITH COIL SEGMENTS

🐝🐝 Length: 16 inches (40 cm) without clasp

MATERIALS AND TOOLS

3-mm mandrel

8 ¼ feet (2.5 m) of sterling silver wire, 18 gauge (1 mm)

10 inches (25 cm) of sterling silver wire, 18 gauge (1 mm)

50 rings made from 14-gauge (1.5 mm) sterling silver wire on a 5-mm mandrel

Sterling silver lobster claw clasp, 15 mm

Photo on page 14

Wind a coil with the longer length of wire. Divide this into three segments: one 2-inch (5 cm) coil and two 1 ¼-inch (3 cm) coils. Thread each onto a piece of wire, and form an end eye close to each end of the coil, making them just large enough that the coil can't slip off. Assemble the coils with a ring between each of the segments. Bend the coils (and the wire inside them) to match the curve of the neck. Assemble a chain 9 ¼-inches (23 cm) long, attaching them one to one and to the ends of the coil unit. Mount the clasp.

BRACELET WITH LARGE LOBSTER CLAW CLASP

🐝🐝🐝 Length: 6 ⅞ inches (17 cm) without clasp

MATERIALS AND TOOLS

2.5-mm mandrel

6 ⅝ feet (2 m) of sterling silver wire, 20 gauge (.8 mm)

8 inches (20 cm) of sterling silver wire, 12 gauge (2 mm)

Sterling silver lobster claw clasp, 20 mm

Photo on page 15

Wind a coil with the 20-gauge (.8 mm) wire. Oxidize it.

Make an end eye in one end of the 12-gauge (2 mm) wire.

Shape the wire around a bracelet mandrel.

Turn the coil onto the 12-gauge (2 mm) wire. Find the right length, snip, and finish the open end with an end eye.

Mount the lobster claw clasp on one eye and polish the piece.

BRACELET WITH COIL BEADS

Length: 8 inches (20 cm) without clasp

MATERIALS AND TOOLS

Coil Beads

2-mm mandrel
16 ½ feet (5 m) of sterling silver wire,
22 gauge (.6 mm)

Heavy Coil

5-mm mandrel
10 feet (3 m) of sterling silver wire,
14 gauge (1.5 mm)
Sterling silver ring clasp, 22 mm

Photo on page 14

Make five slender coils from 3 ⅓ feet (1 m) of 22-gauge (.6 mm) wire. Oxidize these.

Cut the 14-gauge (1.5 mm) wire and make some coil beads: three 14 inches (35 cm) long, with the slender spiral starting ⅝ inch (1.5 cm) in from the end, and two 8 ¾ inches (22 cm) long, with the slender spiral starting ¼ inch (0.5 cm) in.

Flip up the outside circles of each bead into eyes centered on the coil and assemble with the short segments at the two ends. Mount the clasp.

Finish the project by polishing it.

COIL RINGS

These rings, shaped as coils around a ring mandrel, are simple and easy to make.

The coils can be cut into single or double rings.

Decorate them with oxidized coils or let the metal speak for itself.

On a ring mandrel, at a point 1 to 2 mm smaller than the correct ring size, wind the wire with your fingers into a spiral. Better a little too small than a little too big. It's easiest to wind the wire when it's about 20 inches (50 cm) long and you're making coils for several rings at the same time. You'll also waste less expensive silver wire, as you'll have more to hold on to.

MATERIALS

Single Ring

3 ¼ inches (8 cm) of sterling silver wire,
12 gauge (2 mm)

Double Ring

6 ½ inches (16 cm) of sterling silver wire,
14 gauge (1.5 mm), or 6 ⅞ inches
(17 cm) of sterling silver wire, 12 gauge
(2 mm)

Photos on pages 14, 15, 21, and 73

Single Ring

With a good wire cutter, cut the coil at the point where the ends will just pass each other. File the ends.

To harden it, pound the ring lightly with a plastic hammer while it's still on the mandrel.

Double Ring

With a good wire cutter, snip the coil where two turns just pass each other. File the ends. Pound the ring lightly with a plastic hammer while it's still on the mandrel to harden it. Be careful that the ring doesn't get too big.

Coils as Decoration on a Ring

Use a mandrel 0.5 mm larger in diameter than the wire the ring is made of so that it will be easy to twist onto the ring. If you want to add color, remember to oxidize the slender coil before twisting it onto the ring.

When coils are used as smaller units they can be attached together, or beads or rings can be mounted between them. Suddenly, something brand new emerges before your eyes.

In this section, you'll use the same tools and the same materials as in the preceding sections.

MAKING RINGS

Place one side of the round-nose pliers into the coil. Hold it firmly with the pliers and "break" the coil.

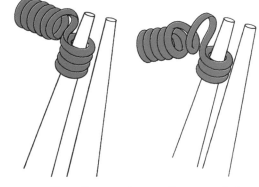

Move the round-nose pliers one circle farther out on the coil. Break the coil again so that the circle that will be snipped apart is separated from the others. Snip it apart with wire cutters.

Finishing a Coil

See the text and diagram on page 11.

BEADS TIED INTO WIRE

A string of beads is always smart. If the string is broken up and the beads are used one at a time, each one is emphasized. If the beads are tied, one by one, into wire, they're enhanced even more.

The technique you'll use depends on the thickness of the wire.

28- to 20-gauge (.3- to .8-mm) wire

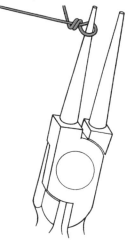

Make an end eye around one tine of the round-nose pliers. Pinch the sharp end against the wire.

Thread the bead onto the wire.

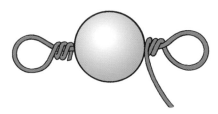

Wrap the wire around the tine of the round-nose pliers about ¼ inch (.5 cm) from the bead, and make a second end eye.

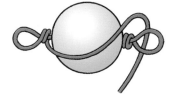

Remove the pliers and hold the bead in your fingers. Bring the wire around the bead and down around the first end eye.

Bring the wire up around and over the first eye, around the opposite side of the bead, and finish by fastening it to the stem of the second end eye.

If more beads are on the wire, turn the wire over and around each before finishing, crisscrossing the first wire.

18- to 16-gauge (1- to 1.2-mm) wire

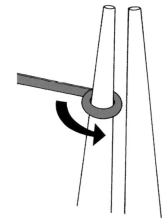

A short way onto the tine of the round-nose pliers, form the wire into an eye.

Remove the pliers and use them to grasp the neck where the eye starts, as shown. Give the eye a little bit of a turn in the opposite direction from the eye to center it perfectly on the wire.

Place the bead on the wire close to the eye. About ¼ inch (.5 cm) from the bead, make another, identical eye. Snip off the excess wire.

NECKLACE WITH GOLD BEADS

 Length: 15⅝ inches (39 cm) without clasp

MATERIALS AND TOOLS

3.5-mm mandrel

3⅓ feet (1 m) of half-round sterling silver wire, 2 x 1 mm

3⅓ feet (1 m) of sterling silver wire, 18 gauge (1 mm)

Sterling silver spring ring clasp, 15 mm

14 gold beads, 14 carat, 5 mm in diameter

Photo on page 21

Make the coil with the half-round wire. Oxidize the coil, the 18-gauge (1 mm) wire, and the clasp. Breaking up the coil: With round-nose pliers, "break" the coil between circles 4 and 5 and then between circles 3 and 4. Snip them apart. Continue to do this until you have no coil left. Flip up the ends of all the segments and neatly center them over the coil with the ends tucked in. Put the beads on the remaining wire, making eyes as shown in the drawing at left. Carefully turn the eyes, and join the bead sections to the coil segments. Mount the clasp and polish.

BRACELET WITH GOLD BEADS

 Length: 6⅞ inches (17 cm) without clasp

MATERIALS AND TOOLS

3.5-mm mandrel

1⅝ feet (.5 m) of half-round sterling silver wire, 2 x 1 mm

1⅝ feet (.5 m) of sterling silver wire, 18 gauge (1 mm)

Sterling silver spring ring clasp, 15 mm

6 gold beads, 14 carat, 5 mm in diameter

Photo on page 21

Follow the necklace directions at left to create the bracelet.

CORKSCREW EARRINGS WITH GOLD BEADS

Read about dangle earrings in the section Coils Stretched into Waves, on page 24.

Photo on page 21

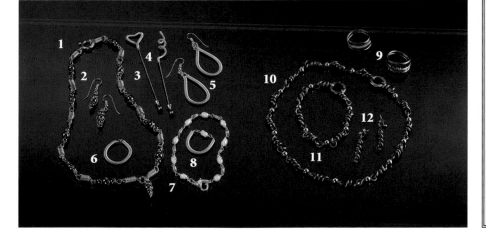

NECKLACE WITH HEMATITE BEADS

 Length: 16 inches (40 cm) without clasp

MATERIALS AND TOOLS

4-mm mandrel

5 feet (1.5 m) of sterling silver wire, 18 gauge (1 mm)

6⅝ feet (2 m) of sterling silver wire, 22 gauge (.6 mm)

22 hematite beads, 3 mm in diameter

11 hematite beads, 5 mm in diameter

Sterling silver spring ring clasp, 12 mm

Photo on page 20

Make the coil with the 18-gauge (1 mm) wire. Coil segments: Break the coil between circles 8 and 9 and again between circles 7 and 8. Snip apart. Flip up the ends of each segment and neatly center them with the ends tucked in. Make 13 segments. Tie in the beads with the 22-gauge (.6 mm) wire. Each group of beads consists of one 3-mm, one 5-mm, and another 3-mm bead. Carefully lift the finished ends of the coils to mount the bead sections. Mount the clasp and polish.

EARRINGS WITH HEMATITE BEADS

MATERIALS AND TOOLS

1⅝ feet (.5 m) of sterling silver wire, 22 gauge (.6 mm)

4 hematite beads, 3 mm in diameter

2 hematite beads, 5 mm in diameter

2 sterling silver French earring wires

Photo on page 20

Each group of beads consists of one 3-mm, one 5-mm, and one 3-mm bead tied together. See the diagrams on page 18.

The eyes on the earring wires can be pried open to mount the bead units to them.

SILVER COIL BRACELET WITH FRESHWATER PEARLS

Length: 7¼ inches (18 cm) without clasp

MATERIALS AND TOOLS

2-mm mandrel

3⅓ feet (1 m) of sterling silver wire, 22 gauge (.6 mm)

9 freshwater pearls, 3 x 5 mm

3⅓ feet (1 m) of .999 fine silver wire, 24 gauge (.5 mm)

2 rings made from 16-gauge (1.2 mm) sterling silver wire on a 4.5-mm mandrel

Heart-shaped sterling silver clasp, 15 mm

Photo on page 20

Make a coil with the 22-gauge (.6 mm) wire.

Coil segments: Break the coil between circles 6 and 7, and once more between circles 5 and 6. Snip them apart.

Flip up the ends of the segment, centering them neatly over the wire with the ends tucked in. Make eight coil units.

Tie the pearls into the soft 24-gauge (.5 mm) wire, as shown on page 18. Carefully lift the ends of the coil units to join them to the tied-in beads.

Attach the two jump rings to the ends of the necklace and mount the clasp on one end.

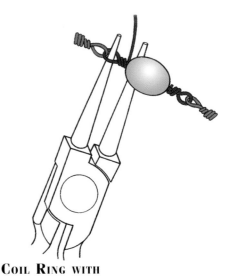

COIL RING WITH FRESHWATER PEARL

MATERIALS AND TOOLS

2-mm mandrel

32 inches (80 cm) of sterling silver wire, 22 gauge (.6 mm)

8¾ inches (22 cm) of .999 fine silver wire, 24 gauge (.5 mm)

1 freshwater pearl, 3 x 5 mm

Photo on page 20

Measure 24 inches (60 cm) of the 22-gauge (.6 mm) wire and make the coil. Measure the length around the finger and snip the coil to the correct length.

The remainder of the 22-gauge (.6 mm) wire is used inside the coil and is finished with an eye at each end. Pinch the ends of the coil in on themselves.

Catch the eyes from the coil into the eyes on each side of the pearl as you perform the tie-in with the fine silver wire.

Coil Ring

MATERIALS AND TOOLS

2-mm mandrel

3 1/3 feet (1 m) of sterling silver wire,
22 gauge (.6 mm)

Photo on page 20

Measure 32 inches (80 cm) of the wire
and make the coil. Measure the length
around the finger and snip the coil to the
correct length. Pinch in the ends.

Make an eye with the remainder of the
wire, and thread it into the coil. Join into
a ring with an eye joining the first eye.
Polish.

Coil Dangle Earrings

MATERIALS AND TOOLS

2-mm mandrel

6 5/8 feet (2 m) of sterling silver wire,
22 gauge (.6 mm)

10 inches (25 cm) of sterling silver wire,
18 gauge (1 mm)

2 rings made from 16-gauge sterling silver
wire on a 4.5-mm mandrel

2 sterling silver French earring wires

Photo on page 20

Make the coil from the 22-gauge (.6 mm)
wire and divide it into two equal pieces.
Make an eye in one end of the 18-gauge
(1 mm) wire. Thread it through one coil,
then pinch the ends of the coil. Thread
the free end of the 18-gauge (1 mm) wire
through its first eye and end with another
eye. Pinch the first eye so that it lies flat.
Mount a jump ring through the eye and
mount it on the earring wire. Make the
other earring the same way. Polish.

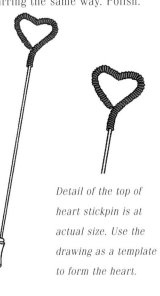

Detail of the top of
heart stickpin is at
actual size. Use the
drawing as a template
to form the heart.

Heart Stickpin

MATERIALS AND TOOLS

2.25-mm mandrel or U.S. size 1
knitting needle

1 5/8 feet (.5 m) of sterling silver wire,
24 gauge (.5 mm)

Stickpin

Photo on page 20

Make the coil. Shape the end of the stickpin using the drawing at left as a template. Turn the coil onto the stickpin and
pinch in the ends.

Spiral Stickpin

MATERIALS AND TOOLS

2.25-mm mandrel or U.S. size 1
knitting needle

20 inches (50 cm) of sterling silver wire,
24 gauge (.5 mm)

Stickpin

4-mm mandrel

Photo on page 20

Make the coil with the 24-gauge (.5 mm)
wire on the knitting needle.

Shape the stickpin into an open coil on
the 4-mm mandrel.

Turn the coil onto the stickpin and pinch
in the ends.

Coils Stretched into Waves

This use of coils is entirely different and yet as simple as can be. Pulling the spiral apart provides a completely new basic material with new characteristics. You can make circles and squares from this new form. You can make webwork magic by binding wires back and forth across it. And you can decorate it with beads. It's up to you to create your own style.

The tools and materials are the same as in the section Coils on Coils, on pages 11 and 12.

STRETCHING COILS

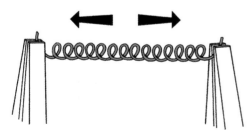

Make the coil as described on page 11.

With two flat-nose pliers, hold the outermost circles of the coil. Pull the pliers apart, either until the wire is the right length or until it's wavy enough for your design.

CORKSCREW EARRINGS

MATERIALS AND TOOLS

2-mm mandrel

6 inches (15 cm) of sterling silver wire, 18 gauge (1 mm)

2 sterling silver French earring wires

Photo on page 27

Make the coil and draw it out to 4 inches (10 cm). Cut the coil into two equal lengths. Make an end eye at the end of each length; see the diagram and directions on page 16. File the free ends a little. Mount the pieces on the earring wires.

CORKSCREW EARRINGS WITH GOLD BEADS

MATERIALS AND TOOLS

3.5-mm mandrel

10 inches (25 cm) of half-round sterling silver wire, 2 x 1 mm

20 inches (50 cm) of .999 silver wire, 24 gauge (.5 mm)

8 flat gold roundel beads, 3 x 5 mm

2 gold earring studs, 8 carat

Photo on page 21

Make the coil with the half-round wire and draw it out to 3¼ inches (8 cm). Divide the coil into two equal pieces. File the ends a little so that they don't scratch. Make an eye in one end of each piece (see page 16). Oxidize the coils and the fine wire. Wind the fine wire around the start of the coil. The beads are strung onto the fine wire and are locked in place by winding the wire around the coil before each bead, so that the beads are fastened in between the turns of the corkscrew. Mount the studs into the eyes.

HOOP EARRINGS WITH COILS

MATERIALS AND TOOLS

2-mm mandrel

20 inches (50 cm) of half-round sterling silver wire, 2 x 1 mm

2 hoop earrings

Photo on page 26

Make the coil and oxidize it.

Draw the coil out to 8¾ inches (22 cm) in length. Cut it in two equal lengths. Turn one spiral onto each earring hoop.

Pinch the ends in. Do this carefully, as hoop earrings are usually hollow and can be easily crushed.

NECKLACE WITH WAVY WIRE PENDANT

   Length: 16¾ inches
(42 cm) without clasp

MATERIALS AND TOOLS

2-mm mandrel

*10 inches (25 cm) of half-round sterling
silver wire, 2 x 1 mm*

*14 inches (35 cm) of ready-made sterling
silver chain*

Sterling silver spring ring clasp, 11 mm

*4 rings made from 18-gauge (1 mm) sterling
silver wire on a 4-mm mandrel*

Photo on page 26

Cut off 4 inches (10 cm) of the wire.
Make the rest into a coil and oxidize it.
Draw out the coil to 3¼ inches
(8 cm). Make an eye in one end of the 4-
inch (10 cm) piece. Turn the oxidized coil
onto it. Pinch the ends of the coil. Finish
the end of the inside wire with another
eye and shape it into a gentle curve.
Mount the chain to the pendant and to
the clasp with jump rings.

JOINING WAVY WIRES

With round-nose pliers, make a hook on
each end of the wire.

Make the hooks grab each other. Pinch
them shut with flat-nosed pliers. Now the
resulting ring can be shaped around a
mandrel or other template.

WAVY CIRCLE EARRINGS

MATERIALS AND TOOLS

2-mm mandrel

*12 inches (30 cm) of sterling silver wire,
18 gauge (1 mm)*

*2 rings made from 18-gauge (1 mm) sterling
silver wire on a 4-mm mandrel*

2 sterling silver French earring wires

Photo on page 27

Make the coil and draw it out to 6½
inches (16 cm). Cut it into two equal
lengths.

Form the circles, as shown at left. Shape
them into a ring on the ring mandrel or
around a thick knitting needle.

Mount the jump rings on one of the
hooked ends of each circle. Mount an
earring wire in each ring.

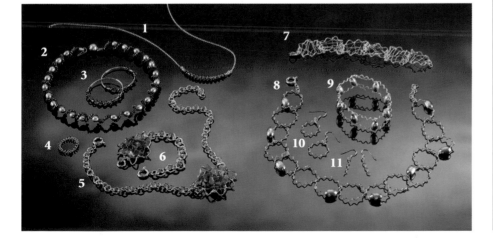

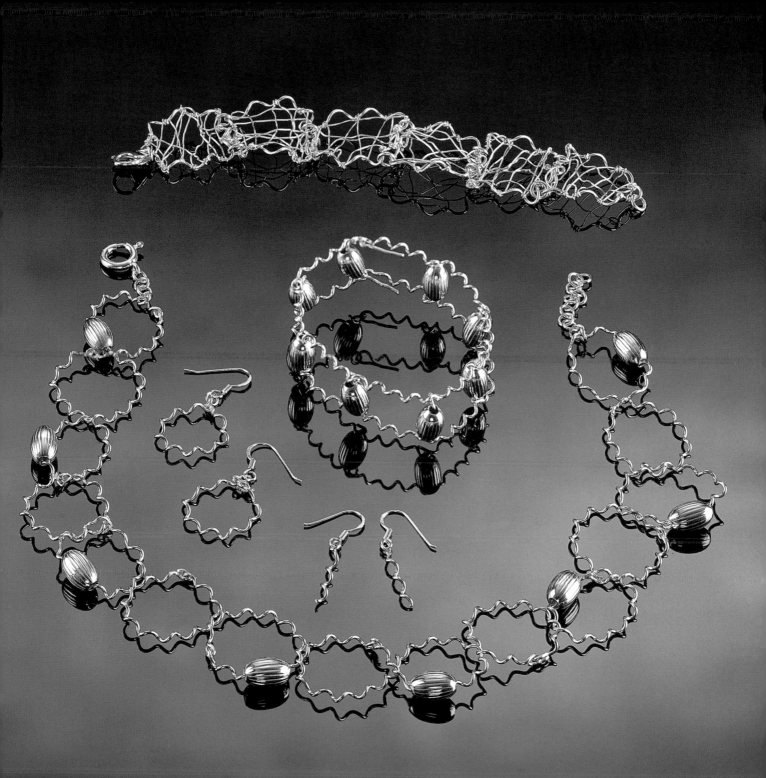

DRAWN-OUT COIL RING

MATERIALS AND TOOLS

2.25-mm mandrel or U.S. size 1
  knitting needle
20 inches (50 cm) of sterling silver wire,
  18 gauge (1 mm)

Photo on page 26

Make the coil and draw it out a little, to
the correct length to fit your finger. Join
the ends with little hooks as described
on page 25. Pinch the ends tight so that
there are no sharp points. Polish.

NECKLACE WITH SILVER NUTMEG BEADS

MATERIALS AND TOOLS

2-mm mandrel
6⅔ feet (2 m) of sterling silver wire,
  18 gauge (1 mm)
8 sterling silver nutmeg beads, 8 mm in
  length
14 rings made from 18-gauge (1 mm) sterling silver wire on a 4-mm mandrel
Sterling silver spring ring clasp, 12 mm

Photo on page 27

Cut the 18-gauge (1 mm) wire into two
3⅓-foot (1 m) lengths. Make the two
coils. Draw each coil out to 28⅞ inches
(72 cm). Cut the drawn-out coils into 3⅝-
inch (9 cm) pieces. Place a bead on one
piece and join it into a ring, as shown on
page 25. Shape the ring on a ring mandrel. Shape the next ring the same way,
but join it to the first ring before closing
the circle. Repeat the fabrication process
until the necklace is long enough. Finish
with jump rings and a clasp. See page 31
for how to assemble the rings. Polish.

BRACELET WITH SILVER NUTMEG BEADS

Length: 7¼ inches
(18 cm) without clasp

MATERIALS AND TOOLS

2-mm mandrel
6⅔ feet (2 m) of sterling silver wire,
  18 gauge (1 mm)
8 sterling silver nutmeg beads, 8 mm
  in length

Photo on page 27

Make the coil and draw it out to 26⅜
inches (66 cm). Cut the wire into seven
3¼-inch (8 cm) pieces and one 3⅝-inch
(9 cm) piece. Place a bead in the center
of the 3⅝-inch (9 cm) piece. Bend the
wire down on both sides of the bead.
Bend the ends of the wire over 1 inch
(2.5 cm) from the bead. This will later
become a primitive clasp. Place a bead in
the middle of a 3¼-inch (8 cm) wire, and
bend the wire down on both sides. Close
to the bead, form an eye at each end that
is attached to the wire of the preceding
bead. (See drawing above.)

Repeat this process until the last bead.
Shape the wire on each side of this last
bead into a slightly larger eye so that
the catch has something to hold on to.
When you're finished, shape the project
on a bracelet mandrel into a comfortable
shape. Polish.

MAKING A WEBWORK ORNAMENT

Starting at any point on the edge, tightly wind the wire around the wavy wire
a few times. Pinch the end in. Repeat
this tie-on whenever you start a new
web wire.

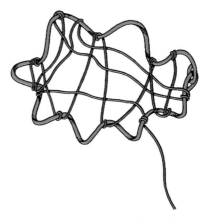

Pull the wire diagonally and wind it
around the opposite edge. Draw the wire
back and forth across the shape until the
square is covered in one direction. Now
weave more wire crosswise to the first

web strands. To stabilize it, wind the wire around the edges fairly often.

To keep them from scratching, remember to pinch the ends of the wire into the wavy wire whenever you begin or end a length of web wire.

BRACELET WITH WEBWORK SQUARES

 Length: 6⅞ inches (17 cm) without clasp

MATERIALS AND TOOLS

2.5-mm mandrel

3⅓ feet (1 m) of sterling silver wire, 16 gauge (1.2 mm)

10 feet (3 m) of .999 silver wire, 24 gauge (.5 mm)

12 rings made from 16-gauge (1.2 mm) sterling silver wire on a 4-mm mandrel

Sterling silver lobster claw clasp, 13 mm

Photo on page 27

Make the coil with 16-gauge (1.2 mm) wire and draw it out to 31¼ inches (78 cm). Cut it into six 5¼-inch (13 cm) pieces. Join each piece into a ring, hooking the ends together as shown in the drawing. Shape them into 1¼-inch (3 cm) squares, using round-nose pliers so as not to mark up the wire. Now fill each square with the fine wire, like spiderwebs, crossing back and forth over them. Lay the squares on a table in such a way that the joints of each square are hidden inside the bracelet. You can pound them with a plastic hammer to ensure that the squares aren't warped.

Join the squares with two jump rings each. You can use flat-nose pliers to adjust the webwork slightly so that the rings lie in the best locations. Set a ring on each end of the assemblage. Mount a clasp on one end. Finally, shape the bracelet around a bracelet mandrel, then polish it.

CARNELIAN PENDANT NECKLACE

 Length: 16¾ inches (42 cm) without clasp

MATERIALS AND TOOLS

5-mm mandrel

12 inches (30 cm) of sterling silver wire, 14 gauge (1.5 mm)

12 carnelian stone beads

24 inches (60 cm) of sterling silver wire, 22 gauge (.6 mm)

25 rings made from 14-gauge (1.5 mm) sterling silver wire on a 5-mm mandrel, for a chain

Sterling silver spring ring clasp, 12 mm

Photo on page 26

I have used fairly heavy wire here, but you can substitute 18- to 16-gauge (1 to 1.2 mm) wire if you wish.

Make the coil with 14-gauge (1.5 mm) wire. Stretch it to 8¾ inches (22 cm)

Make it into a rough shape by bending over the ends (see page 25) and hitching them together.

As you do webwork, thread the beads onto the fine wire and place them randomly, filling the shape with carnelians and silver wire—quite lovely.

Attach a ring on each side of the shape so that the rings are located roughly across from each other and slightly above the vertical center.

Join the rings one by one into two lengths of chain (see page 31 for how to join rings). Mount the clasp on one end of the necklace.

BRACELET WITH CARNELIANS IN WEBWORK

LENGTH: 6⅞ INCHES (17 CM) WITHOUT CLASP

MATERIALS AND TOOLS

5-mm mandrel

12 inches (30 cm) of sterling silver wire, 14 gauge (1.5 mm)

12 carnelian stone beads

24 inches (60 cm) of sterling silver wire, 22 gauge (.6 m)

15 rings made from 12-gauge (2 mm) sterling silver wire on a 6-mm mandrel, for the chain

Sterling silver spring ring clasp, 12 mm

Photo on page 26

Make the coil with 14-gauge (1.5 mm) wire and draw it out to 8¾ inches (22 cm). Join it into a rough shape by bending over the ends (as shown on page 25) and hitching them together. Slip the beads onto the fine wire randomly as you apply webwork to the shape, filling it with carnelians and silver wire. Attach a ring to each side of the shape. Assemble the chain, starting with one of the rings attached to the carnelian structure. The chain ends with the clasp, which grasps the ring on the opposite side of the carnelian structure.

Neck Ring with Gray Freshwater Pearls

Length: 16⅜ inch
(41 cm) without clasp

MATERIALS AND TOOLS

5-mm mandrel

6⅝ feet (2 m) of sterling silver wire,
22 gauge (.6 mm)

6⅝ feet (2 m) of sterling silver wire,
16 gauge (1.2 mm)

5 feet (1.5 m) of sterling silver wire,
24 gauge (.5 mm)

23 gray freshwater pearls, 7 to 8 mm

2 rings made from 18-gauge (1 mm) sterling
silver wire on a 4-mm mandrel

Sterling silver pearl ball clasp, 10 mm

2 sterling silver end pieces,
4 mm in diameter

Photo on page 26

Separately ply the 22-gauge (.6 mm) and the 16-gauge (1.2 mm) wires, until each measures 34 inches (85 cm).

Ply both plied wires together loosely to make one wire. This is the wire you'll work with.

Make a coil on the mandrel, as described on page 11. Oxidize the coil and the 24-gauge (.5 mm) wire, or you can polish the coil in the tumbler.

Draw the spiral out to the proper length.

Be careful not to pull it out too far, or it may spring and entirely lose its coiled character.

Shape the neck ring on something round until you're happy with its shape.

Now add the pearl beads: Start by winding 24-gauge (.5 mm) wire tightly around one end of the neck ring. Place a bead on the wire. Wrap the wire through the next turn of the spiral. Repeat this until all the spaces between turns have pearls. End by wrapping the end of the wire around the coil as you did at the beginning.

Instead of large freshwater pearls, you might use many smaller ones.

Glue on the end pieces (see page 10) and add the clasp.

COILS SAWN INTO RINGS

A popular way to use coils in jewelry making is to saw a coil into rings, and then join them in a variety of patterns using two pairs of chain-nose pliers. Ready-to-use rings (called *jump rings*) can be purchased. It is, however, possible to make your own rings as described in this section.

If you're accustomed to working with this technique, you know that there's usually a link between the project and the thickness of the wire, which is called the "key number." In this book, the ring sizes shown in the photographs are those described in the text. Large rings are combined with smaller ones. You can always change the size of the rings—just play with it. For those of you who have never before tried the chain mail technique, it's better to keep to the recommended sizes.

I used purchased rings for the ornaments shown. If you want to saw your own rings, you should allow a little more material—there is waste in sawing—and be aware that the level of difficulty increases a little.

Tools for the Projects

To open and close the rings you'll need two pairs of chain-nose pliers and, optionally, a rotary tumbler for polishing.

To make your own rings you'll need an eggbeater drill, winding and bracelet mandrels, a vise, a jeweler's saw and blades, two pairs of chain-nose pliers, a piece of soft leather, and optionally, a rotary tumbler.

What Kind of Wire Should Be Used?

Copper, brass, or round or half-round sterling silver.

Silver-plated or colored wire isn't recommended, as the coating will crack off when you work it with pliers.

JOINING RINGS

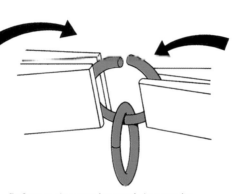

Before a ring can be used, it must be opened with two pairs of chain-nose pliers, turning the ends of the ring away from each other. Put them back together by moving the ends a little beyond each other in the other direction and a bit toward the center of the joint. Then pull ever so slightly on the ring ends and they'll pop together, so that the ring is once more a ring. Never pinch the rings across their diameter or they'll never again be round.

If you're unable to close the ring completely the first time, you'll have to open the ring again before trying once more to close it.

MAKING YOUR OWN RINGS

First make a coil, as shown on page 11.

Sawing Out Rings

Place the mandrel (with the coil on it) in the vise, cushioned with a piece of leather, as shown. This prevents the vise from marking the wire.

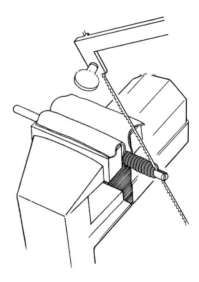

Put the blade in the saw, with the teeth facing the handle. Always use the thinnest possible blade for soft metals. Tighten it well.

Make a little cut into the mandrel first, which you'll use as a miter cut to help steer the blade as you saw.

Saw with gentle up-and-down strokes, without pressing or forcing the saw. Let the saw do the work. Be careful not to cut through the underside of the coil.

Be generous when buying blades, and have plenty on hand if you choose to cut your own rings.

SIMPLE CHAIN OF LARGE AND SMALL RINGS

Put a large ring together.

Put three small rings onto it.

Put another large ring through the three small rings.

Repeat until the chain reaches the correct length.

SIMPLE NECKLACE THREADED WITH SILVER AND GOLD BEADS

Length: 16 ¾ inches (42 cm) without clasp

MATERIALS AND TOOLS

50 rings made from 16-gauge (1.2 mm) sterling silver wire on a 6-mm mandrel

144 sterling silver rings made from 20-gauge (.8 mm) sterling silver wire on a 2.8-mm mandrel

15 sterling silver round beads, 4 mm dia.

5 round .585 gold beads, 3 mm in diameter

Sterling silver heart-shaped clasp, 30 mm

2 rings, one from 18-gauge (1 mm) sterling silver wire on a 2- to 3-mm mandrel, and one from 16-gauge (1.2 mm) wire on a 5- to 6-mm mandrel

Photo on page 35

Assemble the chain, following the drawing at left. Place the beads on randomly as you go along. Mount the clasp on two of the smaller rings. Polish in the rotary tumbler.

TRIANGLE OF PAIRED RINGS

This pattern consists of pairs of rings, always pairing two of the same size.

Assemble two large rings. Set two small rings into them. Continue, as shown above, until you have five pairs of large rings and four pairs of small ones.

In the two large rings on the ends, set a pair of small rings. For the other pairs of large rings, set four small rings in each.

Make six small rings so they're ready. Join a pair of large rings to one of the outermost rings; before closing the large rings add another pair of small rings to them. Set the next pair of large rings into the newest pair of small rings and also into the next two pairs of small rings.

Before closing these large rings, place two more small rings on it. Continue across the row this way.

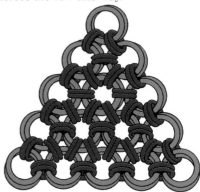

Repeat the process until the triangle is finished.

TRIANGLE PENDANT NECKLACE

Length: 16 ⅜ inches (41 cm) without clasp

MATERIALS AND TOOLS

130 rings made from 18-gauge (1 mm) sterling silver wire on a 5-mm mandrel

166 rings made from 20-gauge (.8 mm) sterling silver wire on a 2.8-mm mandrel

2 rings made from 16-gauge (1.2 mm) sterling silver wire on a 6-mm mandrel

Sterling silver lobster claw clasp, 15 mm

Photo on page 42

Assemble a triangle, following the drawings on this page.

Continue off two corners of the triangle, making a chain like the first side of the triangle, with pairs of large rings joined by pairs of small rings. End with one 16-gauge (1.2 mm) ring on each end and mount the clasp.

Bracelet with Big Diamond Shapes

Length: 7 ¼ inches (18 cm) without clasp

MATERIALS AND TOOLS

90 rings made from 16-gauge (1.2 mm) sterling silver wire on a 4-mm mandrel

270 rings made from 20-gauge (.8 mm) sterling silver wire on a 2.8-mm mandrel

Sterling silver lobster claw clasp, 13 mm

Photo on page 42

Each element of this handsome bracelet consists of two triangles assembled according to the directions on the facing page, then joined along one side. Instead of pairs of large rings, however, single large rings are used. The small rings are still used in pairs.

Assemble six triangles, substituting a large ring each time the directions call for a pair of large rings. Use a row of double small rings along one side to join pairs of triangles into the diamond shapes.

Lay the diamond shapes out in a row on a flat surface. Remove the large rings at the two ends of the diamond shape that will be at the center of the bracelet. Join these leftover small rings to the large rings at the ends of the two end diamond shapes. Set a large ring in each end of the chain of diamond shapes, and mount a clasp in one end.

LATTICE

Here the rings are again used in pairs, two identical rings at a time, every time.

Connect three pairs of large rings with two pairs of small rings, as shown above.

Attach the two outermost pairs of large rings with two small rings. Lay out the assemblage so that it forms a triangle, with one unit pointing down.

Set a pair of small rings in each of the top pairs of rings.

The lattice now lacks only a top ring, which consists of a pair of large rings set in the two pairs of small rings on top. A variation of this lattice pattern is shown on page 36.

Variation on the Lattice Pattern

This is the same pattern, but with only one size ring—still in pairs—used throughout to make the shape, except in the center of each unit, which here is a single ring. (Because of the equal and fairly small size of the rings, the shape almost entirely loses its lattice character.)

SILVER BRACELET OF CHAINED LATTICE

 Length: 17 cm without clasp

MATERIALS AND TOOLS

64 rings made from 18-gauge (1 mm) sterling silver wire on a 5-mm mandrel

80 rings made from 20-gauge (.8 mm) sterling silver wire on a 2.8-mm mandrel

2 rings made from 16-gauge (1.2 mm) sterling silver wire, to support the clasp

Heart-shaped sterling silver clasp, 15 mm

Photo on page 35

Assemble eight lattice shapes, as shown on page 33. Join the lattices with a pair of small rings. Set the 16-gauge (1.2 mm) rings on both ends of the assemblage and mount the clasp on one end.

LATTICE BRACELET WITH HEMATITE RINGS

 Length: 7 ¼ inches (18 cm) without clasp

MATERIALS AND TOOLS

117 rings made from 16-gauge (1.2 mm) sterling silver wire on a 4.5-mm mandrel

8 hematite rings, 13 mm in diameter

Sterling silver spring ring clasp, 15 mm

Photo on page 34

The lattices for this bracelet are assembled following the variation described at left. The round hematite rings and the ring clasp have almost the same diameter and seem almost to be created for this pattern.

Assemble a lattice figure, substituting a hematite ring for the fourth ring in the last stage of the process, as described on page 33.

The next lattice figure starts and ends with the hematite ring. The latticework between the pairs of hematite rings has 13 silver rings.

The final lattice figure ends with a silver ring rather than a hematite ring. In this silver ring, set two more rings. Repeat the pattern at the other end and mount the clasp on one end.

Oxidize the clasp. Polish it.

MAKING A DAISY

The daisy consists of two identical rings used in pairs.

Assemble two large rings. Set 12 small rings on this pair of rings, as above.

Close 12 small rings so they are ready. Set a pair of large rings in two of the 12 small rings already set. Before closing the large ring, set two pairs of small rings onto it. The next pair of large rings is set on both two small rings from the second large ring and two small rings from the first large ring. Before you close the third pair of large rings, put two more small rings onto them. Continue this all the way around. The last pair of large rings is attached to the center by two small rings and to the first "petal" by the two small rings already there.

Variation on a Daisy

Assemble according to directions for Making a Daisy. Start with a pair of large rings in the center, but for the petals, use only one slightly larger ring instead of pairs of large rings.

DAISY CHAIN WATCHBAND

 Length: 5 ¼ inches (13 cm) without clasp or watch

MATERIALS AND TOOLS

40 rings made from 18-gauge (1 mm) sterling silver wire on a 5-mm mandrel

152 rings made from 20-gauge (.8 mm) sterling silver wire on a 2.8-mm mandrel

Watch

Sterling silver lobster claw clasp, 15 mm

Photo on page 34

Measure your watch and the wrist you want to wear this piece. The watch shown here fits by ending with two nearly complete daisies. The number of daisies and partial daisies will vary with every wrist and every watch. On each side of a watch, for mounting, is a rod that works like a toilet paper roller. The easiest way is to set a few small rings around this rod without removing it. If you do remove it, and you lose it, you can usually buy a replacement. Make four daisies following the pattern. Join the daisies two by two with two small rings on each end. Assemble the (partial) daisies that fit the sides of the watch and attach them to the watch. Join the other daisies to them, two to a side. Finish the watch chain with a heavier ring on each side. Mount the clasp in one.

BRACELET WITH HEART CLASP

 Length: 6 ½ inches (16 cm) without clasp

MATERIALS AND TOOLS

98 rings made from 20-gauge (.8 mm) sterling silver wire on a 2.8-mm mandrel

49 rings made from 16-gauge (1.2 mm) sterling silver wire on a 4-mm mandrel

16 rings made from 18-gauge (1 mm) sterling silver wire on a 5-mm mandrel

Sterling silver heart-shaped clasp, 20 mm

Photo on page 43

This bracelet is made using the Variation on a Daisy, as described above.

Assemble seven daisies. Join them into a chain with pairs of small rings. Set one ring into each end for the clasp. Mount the clasp.

TWO-BY-TWO RINGS IN LONG ROWS

This pattern consists of rings used in pairs.

Join two pairs of large rings with a pair of small rings. If you were to continue in this way, you would get a long chain that could be assembled into triangles and squares. See the variations at right.

Close a handful of small rings and have them ready. Set two pairs of small rings into each pair of large rings. Set a pair of large rings into the outside pair of small rings on one side. Slip two small rings onto each pair of large rings before closing them. Join the next pair of large rings to the two new small rings and the next pair of small rings from the first row. Slip two small rings onto this pair of large rings before closing them. The final pair of large rings in the row is joined to the new pair of small rings and to the last pair of small rings from the first row.

The next row is only small rings set onto the pairs of large rings from the last row—one pair for each of the outside rings and two pairs in the center ring.

The rows that follow alternate three pairs of large rings with two pairs of large rings. Repeat the process.

Variation on Two-by-Two

The variation is assembled in the same order, but for the pair of large rings, substitute a single ring made from 16-gauge (1.2 mm) sterling silver wire formed on a 4-mm mandrel.

WIDE BRACELET WITH DOUBLE CLASP

 Length: 5¼ inches
(13 cm) without clasp

MATERIALS AND TOOLS

Sterling silver double clasp, 30 mm

224 rings made from 20-gauge (.8 mm) sterling silver wire on 2.8-mm mandrel

94 rings made from 18-gauge (1 mm) sterling silver wire on 5-mm mandrel

Photo on page 35

In the end piece of each side of the clasp is a crosspin. Set four small rings on each of these.

Start the bracelet in the rings on the end piece. Assemble it by following the basic two-by-two pattern. Finish the bracelet by setting the final two rings into the small rings on the other end piece.

BRACELET WITH TWO-IN-ONE-IN-ONE DIAMONDS

Here large rings are joined with two small rings between them.

 Length: 7¼ inches
(18 cm) without clasp

MATERIALS AND TOOLS

45 rings made from 2 x 1-mm half-round sterling silver wire on a 5-mm mandrel

105 rings made from 18-gauge (1 mm) sterling silver wire on a 3.5-mm mandrel

Sterling silver lobster claw clasp, 15 mm

Photo on page 43

First assemble a square consisting of three rows of three large rings joined by setting two small rings between each pair of large rings in all square directions—that is, nine large rings connected by 24 small rings for each square.

Pick two diagonally opposite corners and pull them lightly. Suddenly you have a diamond.

Make five diamonds, and join them lengthwise with two small rings in between. Finish the first and last diamond with two rings for the clasp.

Polish in the rotary tumbler.

BRACELET WITH TWO-IN-ONE-IN-ONE SQUARES

 Length: 7¼ inches
(18 cm) without clasp

MATERIALS AND TOOLS

61 rings made from 2 x 1-mm half-round sterling silver wire on a 5-mm mandrel

172 rings made from 20-gauge (.8 mm) sterling silver wire on a 2.8-mm mandrel

Sterling silver lobster claw clasp, 15 mm

Photo on page 43

Here, large rings are connected with pairs of small rings.

Assemble a square consisting of three rows of three large rings joined by setting two small rings between each two large rings in all square directions—that is, nine large rings connected by 24 small rings for each square. Make six squares.

Join the outside large rings of the center rows of the squares together with two small rings, one large ring, and two small rings. Mount the clasp on one end.

Polish in the rotary tumbler.

Imagine a chain made out of small figure eights. They could be joined lengthwise or horizontally, round or elongated—they can be whatever you want. Use them alone or joined with rings. Suddenly, a completely new form of jewelry is born. Give it a try: it's easy! This technique requires a rotary tumbler for best results, as the figure eights are cut with wire cutters and could present a lot of sharp ends. Otherwise, the ends of each figure eight must be filed before assembling the piece.

Tools for the Projects

An eggbeater drill, a hook that will fit your drill chuck, a vise, two pairs of narrow flat-nose pliers, two pairs of wide flat-nose pliers, winding mandrels, wire cutters, a long ruler or tape measure, a ring mandrel, a small file, a plastic hammer, and a rotary tumbler.

What Kind of Wire Should Be Used?

You can use all kinds of wire intended for jewelry making, in gauges starting at .8 mm. The figure eights can be hardened before assembly if the wire remains too soft.

MAKING FIGURE EIGHTS FROM COILS

Make a coil.

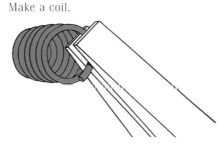

Work the pliers under the end of the first turn of the coil and turn it so that the circle stands up.

With the wire cutters, snip off the next circle; this will become the figure eight.

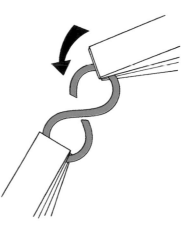

Grasp the figure eight at one end with a pair of pliers. At the same time, tip the other end in place with a second pair of pliers to make a nice figure eight, with the ends as close to the center wire as possible.

Also, open and close the figure eight this way when joining it to something else.

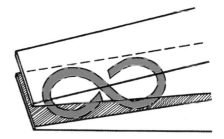

Lay the figure eight in a pair of wide flat-nose pliers and squeeze it lightly so that it's flat and ready to use. When using figure eights in an assembly, face them all in the same direction.

BRACELET OF JOINED FIGURE EIGHTS

 Length: 6 ⅞ inches (17 cm) without clasp

MATERIALS AND TOOLS

3-mm mandrel

3 ⅓ feet (1 m) of sterling silver wire, 18 gauge (1 mm)

1 ring made from 18-gauge (1 mm) sterling silver wire on a 3-mm mandrel

Sterling silver fancy lobster claw clasp, 15 mm

Photo on page 46

Make the coil and cut the figure eights, shaping them as described. To join them, carefully open one end.

Attach a ring and a clasp on one end. Polish in the tumbler.

BRACELET OF FIGURE EIGHTS WITH SILVER BEADS

Length: 7 ¼ inches (18 cm) without clasp

MATERIALS AND TOOLS

4-mm mandrel

3 ⅓ feet (1 m) of sterling silver wire, 18 gauge (1 mm)

15 rings made from 16-gauge (1.2 mm) sterling silver wire on a 4-mm mandrel

15 sterling silver ball beads, 4 mm in diameter

Sterling silver fancy lobster claw clasp, 11 mm

Photo on page 46

Make the coil and cut off the figure eights, shaping them with pliers.

Join the figure eights with the rings,

threading a silver bead on each ring before closing it.

Begin and end the bracelet with a single ring. Mount the clasp on one end.

Polish in the tumbler.

NECKLACE OF SMALL EIGHTS AND RINGS

Length: 16 inches (40 cm) without clasp

MATERIALS AND TOOLS

3-mm mandrel

5 feet (1.5 m) of sterling silver wire, 20 gauge (.8 mm)

100 rings made from 22-gauge (.6 mm) sterling silver wire on a 2.1-mm mandrel

2 sterling silver jump rings, 4 to 5 mm in diameter

Sterling silver fancy lobster claw clasp, 11 mm

Photo on page 46

Make the coil and cut and shape the eights as described. Join them with a pair of small rings. Set a larger ring on each end of the finished chain. Mount the clasp on one end. Polish in the rotary tumbler.

FIGURE EIGHT EARRINGS

Length: 1 ½ inches (4 cm)

MATERIALS AND TOOLS

3-mm mandrel

1 ⅝ feet (.5 m) of sterling silver wire, 20 gauge (.8 mm)

32 rings made from 22-gauge (.6 mm) sterling silver wire on a 2.1-mm mandrel

2 sterling silver ear studs with eyes

Photo on page 46

Make the coil. Cut out and shape the figure eights. Lay two of them aside. For each earring, make a chain of seven figure eights, attaching them together with pairs of rings. Attach four small rings to one side of the center figure eight, and one pair in each loop. Join the last figure eights to these small rings. Attach the top figure eight to the eye on the stud (refer to the drawing above).

Polish in the tumbler.

FIGURE EIGHTS MADE OF HALF-ROUND WIRE

Even more possibilities exist when the figure eights are made with half-round wire. Here it's best to use wide flat-nose pliers. When making the coil, it's important to hold the flat side against the mandrel. Although it's somewhat more difficult to work with half-round wire than with round, you will find that the results definitely repay your effort.

FIGURE EIGHT BRACELET WITH HALF-ROUND WIRE

 Length: 6½ inches (16 cm) without clasp

MATERIALS AND TOOLS

3.5-mm mandrel

3⅓ feet (1 m) of sterling silver wire, 18 gauge (1 mm), for the coil segments

3⅓ feet (1 m) of half-round sterling silver wire, 2 x 1 mm, for the figure eights

Sterling silver fancy lobster claw clasp, 11 mm

Photo on page 46

Coil segments: Make the coil with the 18-gauge (1 mm) wire. Break the coil between circles 3 and 4 and again between circles 2 and 3. Cut on the third circle. You'll need about 14 coil segments, which will be used as rings.

Figure eights: Make the coil with the half-round wire and cut and shape the figure eights; you'll need about 13 of them.

When assembling the necklace, it's best to open the figure eights and thread the coil segments onto them.

For the clasp, set a smaller coil segment on the final figure eight at each end. These final coils are broken between circles 2 and 3 and again between 1 and 2. Cut through the second circle.

Polish in the rotary tumbler.

WIDE FIGURE EIGHT BRACELET

 Length: 6½ inches (16 cm) without clasp

MATERIALS AND TOOLS

3.5-mm mandrel

6⅝ feet (2 m) of half-round sterling silver wire, 2 x 1 mm

115 rings made from 18-gauge (1 mm) sterling silver wire on a 3-mm mandrel

Fancy sterling silver lobster claw clasp, 15 mm

Photo on page 47

Make the coil and cut off and shape 50 figure eights.

When assembling the bracelet, *always* face the figure eights in the same direction. (In this case, they all look like S's.) Assemble, following the drawing above. The figure eights that will hold the clasp are set onto the center of the last figure eight, turned lengthwise on the bracelet. Polish in the rotary tumbler.

Bracelet of Rings and Coil Segments

 Length: 6½ inches
(16 cm) without clasp

MATERIALS AND TOOLS

Coil Segments

4-mm mandrel

*3 ⅓ feet (1 m) of sterling silver wire,
18 gauge (1 mm)*

Rings

*20 rings made from 2 x 1-mm half-round
sterling silver wire on a 6-mm mandrel*

*Sterling silver fancy lobster claw clasp,
12 mm*

Photo on page 46

Coil segments: Make the coil. Break it between circles 4 and 5 and again between circles 3 and 4. Cut on the fourth circle. Pinch the coil ends with a pair of pliers to keep them from scratching.

Assembling with rings: When putting the half-round rings together, use fairly wide flat-nose pliers.

Set single rings between the coil segments, using the coil segments as rings. Mount the clasp on one of the end rings. Polish in the rotary tumbler.

JEWELRY FROM ELONGATED
FIGURE EIGHTS

Now that you can make figure eights, it's natural to want to develop the idea a little and find new ways to use them. It's nice to have multiple possibilities available using the same basic techniques. You'll use the same tools and materials as in the section on Coils Snipped into Figure Eights.

Once more, it's important to have a rotary tumbler for polishing, as the figure eights have sharp edges from the wire cutters.

MAKING ELONGATED FIGURE EIGHTS

When you make the coil, use two mandrels. What does this do?

You will get an oval coil (see the drawing at right), which you can cut into elongated figure eights. Join them with single rings or coil segments, with or without

beads or stones.

If you're working with half-round wire, the oval should be turned up a little more before cutting the wire. It's fairly simple to make nice figure eights as described on page 39.

Important

Never wind more than 3 ⅓ feet (1 m) of wire at a time.

SIMPLE BRACELET WITH ELONGATED EIGHTS

Length: 6 ⅞ inches (17 cm) without clasp

MATERIALS AND TOOLS

2 mandrels, 3.5 mm in diameter

3 ⅓ feet (1 m) of half-round sterling silver wire, 2 x 1 mm

9 rings made from 16-gauge (1.2 mm) sterling silver wire on a 4-mm mandrel

Sterling silver fancy lobster claw clasp, 12 mm

Photo on page 46

Make the coil on the two mandrels. Cut and form the figure eights.

Join the eights with the rings. The bracelet starts and ends with one ring.

Mount a clasp on one end.

BRACELET WITH SET STONES

Length: 6 ⅞ inches (17 cm) without clasp

MATERIALS AND TOOLS

2 mandrels, 3.5 mm in diameter

3 ⅓ feet (1 m) of sterling silver wire, 16 gauge (1.2 mm)

18 rings made from 20-gauge (.8 mm) sterling silver wire on a 2.8-mm mandrel

2 sterling silver jump rings for the clasp, 5 mm in diameter

Sterling silver heart-shaped clasp, 10 mm

9 crystal set stones, 6 to 7 mm

8 ¼ feet (2.5 m) of sterling silver wire, 24 gauge (.5 mm)

Photo on page 46

Make the coil with 16-gauge (1.2 mm) wire on the two mandrels. Cut the coils and shape them into eights. You can make approximately 22 for every 3 ⅓ feet (1 m) of wire.

Join the finished eights with pairs of 20-gauge (.8 mm) rings between them. It's important for all the eights to lie the same way.

Set a 5-mm ring on each end and the clasp on one end.

Polish in a tumbler before adding the set stones.

In the middle of each figure eight, mount a set stone. Bind it on with the 24-gauge (.5 mm) wire. It's important to pinch the wires in so they won't scratch the wearer.

EARRINGS WITH SET STONES

MATERIALS AND TOOLS

20 inches (50 cm) of .999 silver wire, 24 gauge (.5 mm)

2 crystal set stones, 6 to 7 mm

2 sterling silver earring studs with eyes

Photo on page 46

Make an eye with the 24-gauge (.5 mm) wire, as described on page 18. Insert the long end of the wire down through the setting, past two posts, then turn and bring it up again through the next hole in the setting, as shown below. Secure the wire around the eye. Pinch the end in closely. Mount the earring by opening the eye on the ear stud.

RING WITH SET STONE

MATERIALS AND TOOLS

4 inches (10 cm) of sterling silver wire, 12 gauge (2 mm)

1 crystal set stone, 6 mm in diameter

20 inches (50 cm) of .999 silver wire, 24 gauge (.5 mm)

Photo on page 46

Shape a ring from the 12-gauge (2 mm) wire on a ring mandrel. One end is turned outward with round-nose pliers. Check for fit afterward.

Bring the end of the ring that isn't sticking out to meet the other side of the ring.

File the ends with a small file. Before tying on the stone, polish it in the tumbler.

Tie the setting onto the curve of the ring by wrapping fine wire around the ring several times on each side of the set stone.

JOINING FIGURE EIGHTS ON EDGE WITH RINGS

You can use figure eights that are round or elongated for this technique. The rings join the eights at the waist. Remember, especially here, that all the eights should face the same way.

To assemble the unit, lay two figure eights on top of each other. Open a ring and set it through one side of the eights, under the middle and up through the opposite loop of the eight. Close the ring.

Continue to lay each eight over the preceding one and join them.

BRACELET OF ELONGATED EIGHTS

 Length: 7 ¼ inches (18 cm) without clasp

MATERIALS AND TOOLS

2 mandrels, 2 mm in diameter

6 ⅝ feet (2 m) of sterling silver wire, 18 gauge (1 mm)

54 rings made from 18-gauge (1 mm) sterling silver wire on a 3-mm mandrel

Sterling silver fancy lobster claw clasp, 12 mm

Photo on page 47

Use 3 ⅓ feet (1 m) of wire at a time to make coils around the two mandrels. Snip the eights out and shape them. You'll need 54.

Assemble them as described at left. Finish each end with a ring. Set a second ring in each end and mount the clasp on one end.

Polish in the rotary tumbler.

BRACELET OF HALF-ROUND WIRE

 Length: 7 ¼ inches (18 cm) without clasp

MATERIALS AND TOOLS

3.5-mm mandrel

3 ⅓ feet (1 m) of half-round sterling silver wire, 2 x 1 mm

35 rings made from 16-gauge (1.2 mm) sterling silver wire on a 6-mm mandrel

2 rings made from 18-gauge (1 mm) sterling silver wire on a 4- or 5-mm mandrel

Sterling silver lobster claw clasp, 12 mm

Photo on page 47

Make a coil of round (not elongated) eights. Cut off and shape them (see page 39).

Assemble the eights with the large rings, as shown in the drawing at left.

Finish both ends with a large ring. In each of these, set a small ring. Mount the clasp on one end.

Polish in the tumbler.

BRACELET WITH END PIECES

 Length: 6 inches (15 cm) without end pieces and clasp

MATERIALS AND TOOLS

5-mm mandrel

3 ⅓ feet (1 m) of sterling silver wire, 18 gauge (1 mm)

7 silver ball beads, 4 mm in diameter

4 rings made from 20-gauge (.8 mm) sterling silver wire on a 2.8-mm mandrel for the end pieces

2 sterling silver end pieces

33 rings made from 16-gauge (1.2 mm) sterling silver wire on a 4-mm mandrel

Sterling silver spring ring clasp, 20 mm

Photo on page 47

Make a round coil. Snip and prepare the figure eights (see page 39).

Set beads on some of the eights.

Set the small rings on the crosspins inside the end pieces. Mount a figure eight in the small rings in one end piece and work from there, assembling the bracelet with eights and 16-gauge (1.2 mm) rings as shown at left.

When the bracelet is long enough, finish by joining the last figure eight to the small rings on the opposite side of the end piece. Mount the clasp. Polish in the rotary tumbler.

RINGS AND PEARLS

Adorning oneself with beads is hardly new, and adorning oneself with elegantly linked chain is ancient. But adornment with beads set into ring chains is a brand new combination. Here I've used simple chain patterns—some a little complicated, some a little heavy, others very light. Use the ones that appeal to you and those you enjoy making. I have used both large and small beads. The largest are the most expensive, but you can also find distinctive and handsome small freshwater pearls in many colors that are not very expensive. It could be that you'll be able to find beads that complement you in color and style. Maybe you have stones or beads tucked away somewhere that you can use in a new way?

The materials and tools are the same as those used in the section Coils Sawn into Rings, on page 31. Beyond that you'll need round-nose pliers.

If the rings are to be polished in a tumbler, it must be done before the chain is assembled. Put the rings on a heavy metal wire loop in the drum. Never tumble-polish pearls or beads.

TYING BEADS INTO WIRE

The wire used in this technique to tie in pearls and other beads is 24-gauge (.5 mm) wire made of .999 fine silver. It's softer and easier to work with than sterling silver (.925). Not all beads have a large enough hole for 24-gauge (.5 mm) wire, but you should use the heaviest wire that will fit. Make an eye with round-nose pliers (see page 16). Thread the bead onto

the wire and slide it down tight to the eye. Wrap the wire tightly up over the bead and finish with a turn or two around the neck of the eye. Pinch in the end. For each project you'll first bind all your beads in wire; then they'll be ready to attach to the rings as you assemble the chain structures.

PLAIN CHAIN

A plain or simple chain is one made of single rings linked one-by-one crosswise on each other. In Scandinavia it's called "anchor chain," as it's a smaller version of the giant chain used for ship anchors. Here we use fairly heavy rings. At right you'll find the measurements of other gauges that can also be used.

To make a 7¼-inch (18 cm) chain you can use rings of the following dimensions: Rings made from 18-gauge (1 mm) wire on a 3-mm mandrel, from 16-gauge (1.2 mm) wire on a 4-mm mandrel, from 16-gauge (1.2 mm) wire on a 4.5-mm mandrel, or from 14-gauge (1.5 mm) wire on a 5-mm mandrel

Photo on page 34

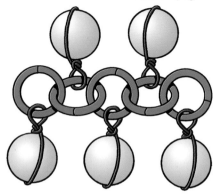

ANCHOR CHAIN BRACELET WITH GREEN, GOLD, AND PEARL BEADS

 Length: 6⅞ inch (17 cm) without clasp

MATERIALS AND TOOLS

60 green, gold, and pearl beads, 4 to 6 mm in diameter

13¼ feet (4 m) of .999 fine silver wire, 24 gauge (.5 mm)

34 rings made from 14-gauge (1.5 mm) sterling silver wire on a 5-mm mandrel

Sterling silver spring ring clasp, 12 mm

Photo on page 52

Tie the beads into the wire. Polish the

rings, if you wish. As you assemble the chain, attach a tied bead to a ring before closing it. The bracelet shown here has two or three beads on each link. Attach the clasp directly to one of the end rings.

EARRINGS WITH BEADS

Length: ⅞ inch
(2 cm)

MATERIALS AND TOOLS

12 pearls, 7 to 8 mm

20 inches (50 cm) of .999 silver wire, 24 gauge (.5 mm)

8 rings made from 14-gauge (1.5 mm) sterling silver wire on a 5-mm mandrel

2 sterling silver earring studs with eyes

Photo on page 52

Tie the pearls into the fine wire. Here I used six pearls for each earring. Polish the rings. Each earring is made of four rings. Set the pearls onto the rings before closing them. Mount the studs directly on the second ring.

FLAT CHAIN MAIL

The chain mail used in medieval armor was made of rings assembled just as they are in this pattern. If a few other techniques are mixed in, a unique jewelry look emerges. Here the chain mail is decorated with pearls, but it's handsome jewelry even without them.

Assemble a group of rings, as shown above, in this pattern: 2 + 1 + 2 + 1 + 2. Lay out the assemblage.

Where there are two rings next to each other at the bottom, join them with another ring. This row is just two new rings.

Join the two new rings with another and set another ring on each side to continue the three-ring series.

Repeat the process until the work is long enough.

See page 54 for wire gauges that can be used for chain mail.

The flat chain mail shown on page 51 can be made of rings in the following dimensions:

20-gauge (.8 mm) wire on a 2.8-mm mandrel

18-gauge (1 mm) wire on a 3.5-mm mandrel

16-gauge (1.2 mm) wire on a 4-mm mandrel

14-gauge (1.5 mm) wire on a 5-mm mandrel

12-gauge (2 mm) wire on a 7-mm mandrel

2 x 1-mm half-round wire on a 6-mm mandrel

FLAT CHAIN MAIL BRACELET WITH PEARLS

Length: 6 ⅞ inches (17 cm) without clasp

MATERIALS AND TOOLS

12 pearls, 4 x 5 mm, in assorted colors

3 ⅓ feet (1 m) of .999 silver wire, 24 gauge (.5 mm)

26 rings made from 18-gauge (1 mm) sterling silver wire on a 3.5-mm mandrel

Sterling silver lobster claw clasp, 10 mm

Photo on page 53

Tie the pearls into the fine wire. Polish the rings if desired.

Assemble the bracelet according to the directions for flat chain mail on page 51.

Attach the pearls as you go along or, if you prefer, assemble the bracelet first, then open individual rings and attach the pearls.

Mount a clasp on the end rings.

WIDE BRACELET WITH LARGE PEARLS

Length: 7 ¼ inches (18 cm) without clasp

MATERIALS AND TOOLS

150 rings made from 2 x 1-mm half-round sterling silver wire on a 6-mm mandrel

47 pearls 8 x 12 mm

10 feet (3 m) of .999 silver wire, 24 gauge (.5 mm)

Sterling silver spring ring clasp, 20 mm

Photo on page 53

Polish the rings. Prepare the pearls by tying them into wires. Follow the basic pattern for assembling the chain mail. When working with half-round wire, use wider flat-nose pliers. Attach the pearls as you go along. Don't put pearls in the outermost rings on the ends or the sides.

Finish both ends with a ring and one end with a clasp.

DOUBLE FLAT CHAIN MAIL

This is simply flat chain mail with doubled rings—two identical rings side by side, every time. Make this chain with 18-gauge (1 mm) wire shaped over a 5-mm mandrel. If you don't space the sections out with rods, you'll need about 78 rings for a bracelet.

RODS BETWEEN CHAIN MAIL SEGMENTS

Make an eye in the rod and use the round-nose pliers to bend the eye back a little so that it's centered on the rod (see page 16).

DOUBLE CHAIN MAIL BRACELET WITH RODS

Length: 6 ⅞ inches (17 cm) without clasp

MATERIALS AND TOOLS

12 inches (30 cm) of half-round sterling silver wire, 2 x 1 mm

40 rings made from 18-gauge (1 mm) sterling silver wire on a 5-mm mandrel

32 pearls, 5 x 6 mm

6 ⅝ feet (2 m) of .999 fine silver wire, 24 gauge (.5 mm)

Sterling silver fancy lobster claw clasp, 15 mm

Photo on page 53

Cut the half-round wire into six pieces, each 1 ¾ inches (4.5 cm) long. Form them into rods with an eye in each end. Curve them slightly around a bracelet mandrel. Polish the rings and the rods. Prepare the pearl beads by tying them into the fine wire. Assemble the chain segments, following the basic double flat chain mail pattern (see above), and attach pearls as you go along. Finally, attach each rod to a pair of rings. Finish both ends with a single ring. Mount the clasp at one end.

PEARL EARRINGS

MATERIALS AND TOOLS

2 pearls, 8 x 12 mm

*2 sterling silver wire headpins, 22 gauge
(.6 mm), each 1 ½ inches (4 mm) long*

Photo on page 53

Set a pearl on a headpin. With round-
nose pliers, bend the headpin above the
pearl. If the pearl needs to be tighter to
keep it from falling off, use glue. Repeat
for the other earring.

STICKPIN WITH WHITE
FRESHWATER PEARLS

MATERIALS AND TOOLS

*2.25-mm mandrel or U.S. size 1
knitting needle*

10 white pearls 2 x 3 mm

*16 inches (40 cm) of sterling silver wire,
24 gauge (.5 mm)*

Stickpin

Photo on page 53

Mount the mandrel in a hand drill.
Thread the pearls on the wire and clamp
the wire alongside the mandrel into the
drill chuck.

Make the coil, easing the pearls onto the
coil as you go along and putting them
wherever you want.

Twist the coil onto the stickpin. Pinch the
ends of the coil. Adjust the pearls so they
look their best.

STICKPIN WITH GRAY
FRESHWATER PEARLS

MATERIALS AND TOOLS

20 to 25 freshwater pearls

*24 inches (60 cm) of sterling silver wire,
24 gauge (.5 mm)*

*2.25-mm mandrel or U.S. size 1
knitting needle*

Stickpin

Photo on page 53

Thread the pearls onto the wire, twisting
them into the wire as shown in the drawing at right. Put the mandrel and one end
of the wire into the drill chuck.

Carefully make a coil. Remove the coil
from the mandrel and turn it onto the
stickpin. Pinch in the ends of the wire.

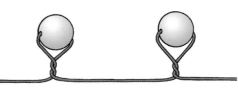

TWISTING BEADS INTO WIRE

Thread the beads onto the wire. Starting
about 1 ¼ inches (3 cm) from one end,
twist on the first bead, as shown. Allow
⅝ inch (1.5 cm) between beads.

Variations

With the same wire and mandrel, try
these easy stickpin ornaments:

Coil Bead

Make a coil from a 28-inch (70 cm) long
wire. Place the coil on a 12-inch (30
cm) long wire and make a new coil (see
page 12).

Double Coil Bead

Make a coil bead. Place it on a 12-inch
(30 cm) long wire and make a new coil
from the bead.

I admire jewelry with wires braided in what seem impossibly complex patterns. But if you take a closer look at the technique, it often turns out that it's not as complicated as it seems. I believe that if you can make woven heart baskets for the Christmas tree or braid hair, you can probably braid wire jewelry.

One important difference is that metal can get fatigued and brittle when it's worked, in the worst cases snapping off entirely. To avoid that, use fine (.999) silver. It's a little more costly, but in this case, necessary. If you don't want to use fine silver, you can substitute finer wire (laid double or tripled) for the wires called for in the directions. The result will be nearly the same.

If a few of the wires are put through the pasta maker, the resulting flat wires will give a touch of interest when mixed with round wires in the braid.

At the same time, the pasta maker will make the wire a little harder, although that doesn't mean as much if you're using fine silver. If you use the pasta maker when making an S-clasp, it will harden the wire and make it stronger.

Materials and Tools for the Projects

You'll need a vise, a piece of soft leather, a plastic hammer, round-nose pliers, two pairs of flat-nose pliers, wire cutters, a pasta maker, a hook that will fit in the chuck of the drill, an eggbeater drill, winding mandrels, ring and bracelet mandrels, a small file, and a block of hardwood drilled with ⅞- to 3¼-inch (2 to 8 mm) holes (see page 9). Use .999 fine silver wire, or colored or plain copper wire.

FINISHING THE BRAID

You will get a smooth, regular surface on your braided piece if you draw it through a wooden block with various size holes before attaching beads to it.

The finished braid can be shaped around almost anything round. A bracelet or ring mandrel is preferable, but anything of the right size will do.

Finally, the finished braid should be lightly pounded with a plastic hammer to achieve the right shape.

FASHIONING THE BRAID INTO A RING

Shape the ring around a ring mandrel, turning the ring so that the flat side of the braid faces the mandrel. Find the right size; better that it's a little too small than too big. The ring can always be enlarged slightly on the ring mandrel.

Take one wire from each end and cut off the other strands close to the braid. Turn and pinch in the ends that are close to the braid. The two remaining wires on each side are sewn into the opposite side, as shown. Before threading the wire in you may need to open a hole with a needle to keep from bending the wire.

COIL SEGMENTS AND S-CLASPS

Sometimes when a piece needs a beautiful finish, it's difficult to find a clasp or end pieces that exactly suit its style and size.

Here are some ways you can make your own end pieces and clasps. Leather cord can also be finished with these.

Choose a mandrel close in diameter to the size of the finished jewelry. The coil will always be slightly larger than the mandrel because of the working of the metal.

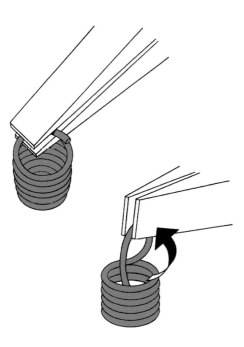

Make the end pieces out of a coil formed on a mandrel, as described on page 11. Grasp the top coil in the middle and lift one end up (as shown at left) to form an eye.

Secure the end coil to the braid (or leather band) by pinching the lowest circle of the coil into the braid with flat-nose pliers.

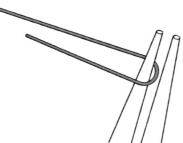

S-Clasp

With round-nose pliers, bend a wire 1½ inches (4 cm) from one end. Bend the wire in the opposite direction, 1½ inches (4 cm) from the first bend, to get a long, flat S-shape (see the clasp in the photo on page 61).

Cut the wire near the first curve. File the ends, perhaps hammering them flat with the plastic hammer. Put the clasp through the pasta maker a few times. Bend the ends up slightly in order to be able to slide it onto the end rings more easily.

BRAIDING THREE STRANDS

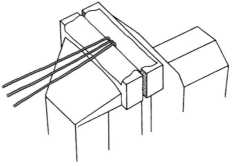

BRAIDED NECKLACE WITH LARGE BEADS

Length: 16 inches (40 cm) without clasp

MATERIALS AND TOOLS

5⅞ feet (1.8 m) of .999 fine silver wire, 24 gauge (.5 mm)

33 glass beads, 6 mm in diameter

2 rings made from 18-gauge (1 mm) sterling silver wire on a 5-mm mandrel

Sterling silver fancy lobster claw clasp, 12 mm

Photo on page 60

Cut the wire into three pieces, each 24 inches (60 cm) long. Clamp them in the vise 2 inches (5 cm) from the ends, using a piece of leather to cushion the wires and keep the vise from marking them. The braid is the normal three-strand braid pattern used for hair. Slide 11 beads onto each wire and secure them there. Start by pushing one bead up when the braided strand is coming from the right. Hold the bead in place while you braid the next wire. Repeat this every second time the braid comes from the right. When the braid reaches the desired length, remove it from the vise. With round-nose pliers, finish with an eye in each end made from the three strands of the braid (see page 18). Set jump rings on the eyes and the clasp in one of them. This braid is soft and lies well. Don't make it too long or it will twist.

Matching Bracelet

If you'd like a bracelet to match the necklace above, use three 12-inch (30 cm) .999 silver wires, 24 gauge (.5 mm), and the same technique.

12-STRAND ROUND BRAID

Divide the wires in two groups of six and clamp them in the vise, cushioned with a piece of leather to keep the vise from damaging the wires.

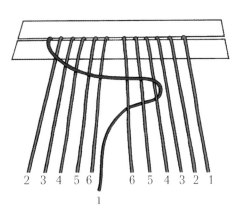

Bring the outside (number 1) wire on the left over all the left-hand wires and three of the right-hand wires, dropping it down between wires 3 and 4 on the right side, then drawing it back to the left-center position.

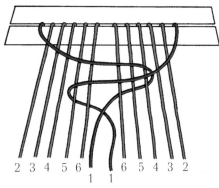

Bring the outside (number 1) wire on the right over all the right-hand wires and over the first three on the left, dropping it between strands 3 and 4 on the left, then bring it back to the right-center position.

Repeat the process until all the wires have been used once, then tighten the braid. The best way to do this is to pull all the strands out sideways and slightly downward at the same time. Finish the braiding, tightening it as described every time you braid a wire.

BRAIDED BRACELET WITH SILVER BEADS

 Length: 6½ inches (16 cm) without clasp

MATERIALS AND TOOLS

10 feet (3 m) of .999 fine silver wire, 18 gauge (1 mm)

3⅓ feet (1 m) of sterling silver wire, 24 gauge (.5 mm)

2 sterling silver end pieces, 5-mm inside diameter

10 sterling silver beads, 4 mm in diameter

Sterling silver spring ring clasp, 20 mm

Photo on page 61

Cut the 18-gauge (1 mm) wire into six 20-inch (50 cm) lengths. Run four of these through the pasta maker. Double the wires over so that you have 12 strands. Clamp the wires in the vise, cushioned with a piece of leather to protect them. Arrange them six to a side. Braid and finish as described above. Cut the braid to the desired length. Oxidize the braid and the 24 gauge (.5 mm) wire. Glue on the end pieces (see page 10). Wait until the glue is completely dry. After securing the 24-gauge (.5 mm) wire to the outside strand of braiding, sew on the silver beads; place them as you wish. Mount the clasp.

Variation of the 12-Strand Braid

Braid around a mandrel with 14 wires instead of 12.

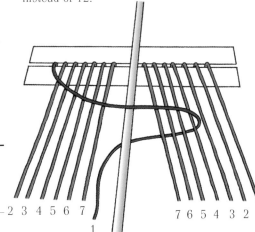

Always bring the outside strand on each side over the other strands and drop it down between strands 3 and 4 on the opposite side. Braid according to the same principles as the 12-strand braid.

OXIDIZED FLAT NECKLACE

 Length: 16 inches (40 cm) without clasp

MATERIALS AND TOOLS

13¼ feet (4 m) of sterling silver wire, 22 gauge (.6 mm)

5 wires of .999 silver, 20 gauge (.8 mm), 4⅝ feet (1.4 m) in length

3.5-mm mandrel

2 sterling silver end pieces, 5-mm inside diameter

Sterling silver lobster claw clasp, 11 mm

6 rings made from 18-gauge (1 mm) sterling silver wire on a 6- or 7-mm mandrel

Photo on page 61

Cut the 22-gauge (.6 mm) wire into two pieces, each measuring 6⅝ feet (2 m). Ply each separately (see page 13).

Put two of the 20-gauge (.8 mm) wires through the pasta maker.

Bend the wires in half. Clamp all 14 in the vise and arrange them with seven to a side. As shown on page 58, lay the mandrel over the vise and braid it by bringing the outside wire from one side over and dropping it between strands 3 and 4 of the opposite side, and so on.

As the braid gets longer, move the mandrel down.

Finishing the Braid

Remove the mandrel. Remove the braid from the vise and lay it on a piece of leather. With a plastic hammer, pound it on two sides of the braid so that it becomes flat and has a regular shape. Determine the desired length and cut off the rest.

Oxidize the braid, the end pieces, the clasp, and the jump rings.

Glue on the end pieces (see Gluing, page 10). When the glue is completely dry, set the jump rings and mount the clasp.

Optionally, polish the piece.

NECKLACE WITH COIL END PIECES

 Length: 16 inches (40 cm) without clasp

MATERIALS AND TOOLS

8 wires of .999 fine silver, 20 gauge (.8 mm), each 4 feet (1.2 m) in length

End pieces and a 1⅗ inches (4 cm) S-clasp

5-mm mandrel

20 inches (50 cm) of half-round sterling silver wire, 2 x 1 mm

8¾ inches (22 cm) of sterling silver wire, 14 gauge (1.5 mm)

Photo on page 61

Run four pieces of 20-gauge (.8 mm) wire through the pasta maker, then randomly place them among the round wires.

Bend all the wires in half and clamp the folded ends in the vise, cushioned with a piece of leather, to make 16 strands. Group them into eight pairs and count each pair as one strand. Put four strands on each side. Braid them as described for the 12-strand braid on page 58, bringing the outer strand over to the opposite side, down between strands 3 and 4, then back to the center on its own side.

Braid to the end and cut off the desired length.

Finish with coiled ends and a clasp, as described on page 57.

More braided jewelry projects on page 62

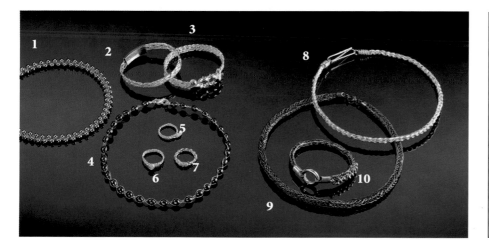

Braided Ring

MATERIALS AND TOOLS

36 inches (90 cm) of .999 fine silver wire,
20 gauge (.8 mm)

Photo on page 60

This braid turns out flat on one side,
which makes it especially well-suited for
rings.

Cut the wire in six 6-inch (15 cm) pieces.
Run four through the pasta maker. Clamp
all the wires in the vise, 1¼ inches (3
cm) in from one end. Divide them into
three groups.

Use the same braiding technique as the
12-strand braid on page 58. Bring the
outermost strand from the left side over
all the left-hand strands and between the
first two wires on the right side, then
back to the left-center position.

Bring the outside strand on the right over
all the right-hand strands, down between
the first two on the left side, then bring it
back to the right side of the center.

Repeat the process, tightening the braid
as you go along.

Pull the whole braid through the wooden
drawing block. See page 56 for how to
assemble the ring.

FLAT BRAID WITH FIVE STRANDS

This technique results in a flat braid;
don't pull it through the drawing block.

When the braid is completed, lay it on
a piece of leather and pound it lightly
with a plastic hammer. Shape it on a ring
mandrel or a bracelet mandrel.

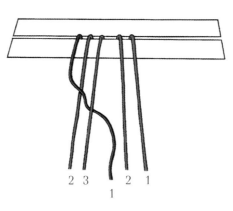

Divide the strands, with three on the left
and two on the right.

Bring the outermost strand on the left
over the center wire and *under* its neighbor; lay it beside the inner wire on the
right side; there are now three strands
on the right.

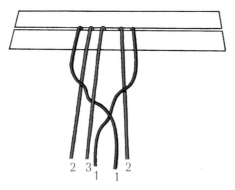

Bring the outermost strand on the right
side *over* its neighbor and *under* the
inner strand on the left side, laying it in
the innermost position on the left side, so
that it again has three strands.

Repeat these two steps. Pull up each
strand firmly as you braid it.

Braided Bangle

 Length: 8 ⅜
inches (21 cm)

MATERIALS AND TOOLS

5 wires of .999 fine silver, 18 gauge (1
mm), 18⅜ (46 cm) inches in length
Flat tube to fit the braid, 4 x 10 mm

Photo on page 60

Bend the wires in half to make 10
strands.

Clamp the folded ends in the vise. Divide
them with six on the left and four on the
right. Group the wires in pairs so that
you are braiding with five double strands.

Braid in the five-strand technique
described at left.

Measure the bracelet around the widest
part of your hand. The ends of the wires
should meet inside the tube so that the
bangle can slip on and off your hand.

Glue the tube onto the braid (see page
10). Optionally, polish the bracelet.

Braided Ring II

MATERIALS AND TOOLS

10 wires of .999 fine silver, 24 gauge (.5 mm), 10 inches (25 cm) in length

Photo on page 60

Bend the wires in half and clamp them in the vise. Divide them, with three pairs on the left and two pairs on the right. Braid with the five-strand technique described for the bangle, above.

Join the ring, as shown on page 56.

Twist the remaining wire around in the middle until it looks like a little rose. Tuck the ends in under the flower.

EIGHT-STRAND FLAT BRAID

Clamp the wires firmly in the vise and divide them into two groups, four to a side.

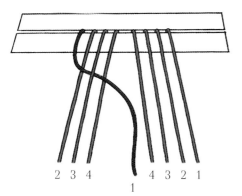

Bring the outermost strand on the left over, under, and over the others in the group and lay it in the middle alongside the innermost strand on the right side, as shown above.

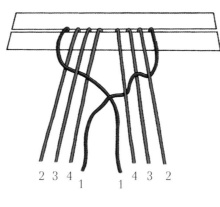

Repeat the same technique with the outermost strand from the right-hand group, laying it *over* the innermost strand on the left hand side.

Bracelet with Double Clasp

Length: 6⅞ inches (17 cm) without clasp

MATERIALS AND TOOLS

8 wires of .999 fine silver wire, 20 gauge (.8 mm), 10 inches (25 cm) in length

8 wires of .999 fine silver wire, 24 gauge (.5 mm), 10 inches (25 cm) in length

2 sterling silver end pieces

Sterling silver double clasp, 35 mm

Photo on page 60

Clamp all the wires in the vise.

Pair up each thin wire with a thick one, and divide them into two groups of four. Braid the wires with the eight-strand braid technique described at left.

Braid until you reach the desired length. Finish by pounding the braid lightly with a plastic hammer. If the end pieces have a cross rod inside, cut them out with wire cutters before gluing the end pieces on (see page 10 about gluing). When the glue is completely dry, mount the clasp.

Adjustable Ring

MATERIALS AND TOOLS

4 wires of .999 fine silver wire, 24 gauge (.5 mm), 12 inches (30 cm) in length

3.5-mm mandrel

Photo on page 60

Bend the wires in half around the mandrel. Clamp the mandrel and the wires in the vise, wrapped in a piece of leather for cushioning so that the vise won't mark the wires.

Divide the wires into two groups of four. Braid 3¼ inches (8 cm). Remove the braid from the mandrel and the vise.

Thread the braided end through the eye created by the mandrel (see drawing, above). Trim all the loose ends close to the braid and pinch them to the underside with flat-nose pliers. The ends should not be visible from the top.

Do you knit or crochet? If the answer is "Yes!" then you can also make jewelry. It feels a little peculiar to work with metal wire instead of yarn, but all you really need is fine enough wire. The best part is, it won't fade or shrink in the laundry.

If you already know that you knit very tightly, then use somewhat thicker knitting needles or a heftier crochet hook than what is called for. There's no gauge given!

Tools for the Projects

You'll need a size B-1 (2.5 mm) crochet hook; U.S. sizes 2, 3, and 4 (2.5- to 3.5-mm) knitting needles; round-nose pliers; wire cutters; two flat-nose pliers; curved needle-nose pliers; a piece of soft leather; and, optionally, a rotary tumbler.

What Kind of Wire Should Be Used?

Use either .999 fine silver wire or colored copper wire, 28 or 26 gauge (.3 or .4 mm).

Finishing

Knitted and crocheted pieces are finished just as if they were made of yarn, by binding off. The difference is that a clasp must be mounted on somehow. The endings can be an actual end piece, which is glued on, or an alternative is to use a coil end piece (see page 57) or a purchased cone-style end piece.

Put a heavier wire into the end of the piece. Work it in and out so it's firmly attached. Trim off the short end.

Thread a cone over the wire, the braid, and the end of the piece. Make an eye in the wire by first grasping the wire ¼ inch (.5 cm) from the end of the cone. Bring the wire around the tine of the pliers and wrap it once or twice around the wire above the cone. Closely nip the wire and pinch in the sharp end with curved needle-nose pliers.

Set a ring in the eye and a clasp in the ring.

MANY CHAINS WITH HEMATITE BEADS

Length: 17 ¼ inches (43 cm) without clasp

MATERIALS AND TOOLS

120 hematite beads, 4 mm in diameter, in both matte and glossy finishes

.999 fine silver wire, 28 gauge (.3 mm)

Size B-1 (2.5 mm) crochet hook

1 ⅝ feet (.5 m) of sterling silver wire, 22 gauge (.6 mm)

2 sterling silver cones, 5 mm in diameter

2 rings made from 18-gauge (1 mm) sterling silver wire on a 4-mm mandrel, for the clasp

Sterling silver fancy lobster claw clasp, 15 mm

Photo on page 66

This chain is made from six separate chains of crochet gathered into the cones at both ends. Each chain holds 20 hematite beads. String 20 beads on the 28-gauge (.3 mm) wire. Crochet chain stitches. Bring a bead up into the chain every fourth stitch. When the chain is long enough, cut the wire and pull the end through to fasten it. Make the other chains the same way, adding beads every fourth stitch, but offset the starting point each time. Fasten each chain, trim the end, and turn it back. Weave the chains together at the ends with 22-gauge (.6 mm) wire and add cones at the ends. Set rings and a clasp in the final eyes.

CROCHETED AND BRAIDED NECKLACE

  Length: 15¼ inches (38 cm) without clasp

MATERIALS AND TOOLS

Size B-1 (2.5 mm) crochet hook

.999 fine silver wire, 28 gauge (.3 mm)

2 sterling silver flat end pieces

2 rings made from 18-gauge (1 mm) sterling silver wire on a 4-mm mandrel, for the clasp

Sterling silver brushed-finish ball clasp, 12 mm in diameter

Photo on page 67

Crochet three chains of chain stitch, each about 18 inches (45 cm) long. Oxidize one chain. Clamp the three chains in the vise and braid them. They can be quite loose. Measure off the right length and snip them with wire cutters. Bind the ends together with a wire by weaving through and around them. Be careful that the weaving doesn't become too bulky to fit into the end pieces. Glue on the end pieces. When the glue is completely dry, mount the rings and the clasp.

CROCHETED AND BRAIDED BRACELET

  Length: 6½ inches (16 cm) without clasp

MATERIALS AND TOOLS

Size B-1 (2.5 mm) crochet hook

.999 fine silver wire, 28 gauge (.3 mm)

2 sterling silver flat end pieces

2 rings made from 18-gauge (1 mm) sterling silver wire on a 4-mm mandrel, for the clasp

Sterling silver brushed-finish ball clasp, 12 mm in diameter

Photo on page 67

Crochet three strands of chain stitches, each 8 inches (20 cm) long.

Finish the same way as the necklace at left.

Knitted and crocheted jewelry can be polished in a tumbler, but preferably before any beads have been woven or knitted in it.

CROCHETED CHOKER WITH PEARLS

  Length: 15⅝ inches (39 cm) without clasp

MATERIALS AND TOOLS

Size B-1 (2.5 mm) crochet hook

.999 fine silver wire, 28 gauge (.3 mm)

25 pearls or crystal chip beads

2 sterling silver end pieces

2 rings made from 18-gauge (1 mm) sterling silver wire on a 4-mm mandrel

Oxidized sterling silver spring ring clasp, 12 mm in diameter

Photo on page 66; two variations on page 67

First row: Crochet a chain 15⅝ inches (39 cm) long. Turn.

Second row: Slip stitch, double crochet, half-double crochet, or treble double, depending on how wide you want the collar. Bind off.

Measure out 6⅝ feet (2 m) of wire for the beads.

All the silver can be oxidized if you wish.

CROCHETED ROSETTES CHOKER

Length: 15¼ inches (38 cm) without clasp

MATERIALS AND TOOLS

Size B-1 (2.5 mm) crochet hook

.999 fine silver wire, 28 gauge (.3 mm)

10 feet (3 m) of .585 gold wire, 28 gauge (.3 mm)

2 rings made from 18-gauge (1 mm) sterling silver wire on a 4-mm mandrel, for the clasp

Sterling silver heart-shaped clasp, 20 mm

Peridot beads

Photo on page 66

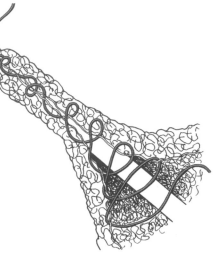

Crochet this piece with a doubled wire.

To make one rosette:

Round 1: Make five chain stitches with the silver wire; form them into a ring with a slip stitch.

Round 2: Make three chain stitches. Make eight double crochet stitches into the ring.

Round 3: One chain stitch, nine single crochet stitches.

Bind off.

Crochet 12 rosettes, including three with an extra round of single crochet.

With wire, weave the rosettes together at the sides, placing the three larger ones in the center.

Oxidize the necklace, the rings, and the clasp.

Weave on the beads with the gold wire.

KNITTED BRACELET WITH PEARLS

Length: 7¼ inches (18 cm) without clasp

MATERIALS AND TOOLS

U.S. size 2 or 3 knitting needles

.999 fine silver wire, 28 gauge (.3 mm)

22 pearl beads, 5 or 6 mm in diameter

6⅔ feet (2 m) of .585 gold wire, 28 gauge (.3 mm)

2 sterling silver flat end pieces

Sterling silver spring ring clasp, 20 mm

Photo on page 66

Cast on 20 stitches with the silver wire. Work the wire in garter stitch (knitting only, no purling). When the bracelet is the right length, bind off. Weave the piece together along the long edge. It's easiest to weave it around a tube. To smooth the surface so it won't scratch in use, first lay it in a piece of soft leather on a table.

Roll and press it at the same time, like rolling sushi in a bamboo mat. Remove the tube. Work the knitting together so that the stitches are on the back.

Oxidize the piece.

Weave on the beads, evenly distributing them, with the gold thread, which should show between them.

Glue on the end pieces.

NECKLACE WITH KNITTED TRIANGLES

Length: 16 inches (40 cm) without clasp

MATERIALS AND TOOLS

U.S. size 4 (3.5 mm) knitting needles

.999 fine silver wire, 28 gauge (.3 mm)

30 faceted hematite beads, 4 mm in diameter

6 rings made from 12-gauge (2 mm) sterling silver wire on a 6-mm mandrel

2 rings made from 18-gauge (1 mm) sterling silver on a 4-mm mandrel, for the clasp

Sterling silver ball catch, 20 mm

Photo on page 67

Knit this piece with a doubled wire.

One Triangle

Cast on 10 stitches and work the wire in garter stitch. Bind off one stitch at the beginning of each row. End the triangle with one stitch, and bind it off. Cut off the end and turn it back into the knitting.

The necklace has six triangles made in this fashion and one that's a little larger, made by casting on 12 stitches instead of 10.

Use the same wire to weave on the beads. Weave a bead on the end of every triangle and scatter the others as you like over all the triangles.

Join the triangles with the large rings, connecting the top corners. Use the knitting needle to work a little hole in each corner for the rings. The large triangle will be in the center. Set the smaller rings on both ends and mount the clasp in one.

This chain can tolerate tumble polishing.

Bracelet with Knitted Squares

 Length: 6 ⅞ inches (17 cm)
without clasp

MATERIALS AND TOOLS

U.S. size 4 (3.5 mm) knitting needles

.999 fine silver wire, 20 gauge (.3 mm)

16 hematite beads, 4 to 5 mm in diameter

*24 rings, made from 16-gauge (1.2 mm)
sterling silver wire on a 4-mm mandrel*

*3 sterling silver lobster claw clasps, 11 mm
each*

Photo on page 67

Knit this piece with a doubled wire.

To knit one square: Cast on 12 stitches and work the wire in garter stitch. Bind off when the work measures 1 ⅜ inch (3.5 cm).

Make three squares in this way.

Weave on the beads, using the same wire. Join the squares with three rings to a side.

Finish both ends with three rings and, on one end, mount the clasps in the rings.

In this section, both new and previously covered techniques are used for additional projects. Everything in this section can be made inexpensively.

Beads, pearls, and stones always inspire me to make jewelry—not necessarily expensive creations that will last for 20 years, but here-and-now jewelry that suits my mood and clothing on a particular day. In this section, we'll also work with tiger tail. People who have done beadwork jewelry are quite familiar with it.

Some techniques are time consuming and some are quick. When you get the hang of jewelry making, try mixing materials and techniques—you'll never run into anyone with exactly the same piece of jewelry.

Finishing is particularly important when you're making lightweight jewelry. It can make all the difference as to whether you're happy with the piece.

Remember always to use wires specifically designed for jewelry making. It's easy to pick up a nickel allergy and almost impossible to get rid of it.

Tools for the Projects

Use two pairs of flat-nose pliers, one pair of round-nose pliers, wire cutters, a vise, a plastic hammer, a piece of soft leather, a long ruler or tape measure, a small file, and a cone or ring mandrel.

Materials for the Projects

Use tiger tail and nylon thread (monofilament); any form of tiger tail in the same thickness given in the patterns; and various end pieces and clasps that are suitable for jewelry making.

ENDINGS FOR WIRE AND MONOFILAMENT

It's important that the end of the wire is hidden so that it doesn't scratch the wearer, but also so that it has an attractive finish. Here are a few possibilities.

End with a short chain of rings on both sides of the clasp. In this way, the length can always be adjusted to suit the wearer of the piece.

Ending a Single Strand with a Bead

Set a crimp bead on the monofilament without closing it. Bend the line back and through the crimp bead to form an eye.

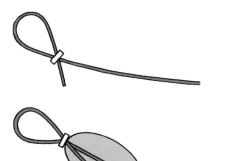

Close the crimp bead. Slide a bead up to the closed crimp bead and set another crimp bead just behind it. Both ends can be finished the same way.

Ending Several Strands with a Bead

Set a crimp bead over all the strands. Pinch it closed about 1¼ inches (3 cm) from the end. One strand will be used for a loop. The others are trimmed about ¼ inch (.5 cm) from the crimp bead.

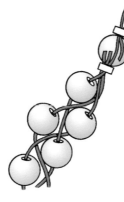

Set a bead on the long strand to hide the cut ends. Place a crimp bead without closing it entirely, just beyond the bead. Bend the wire end back and thread it through the crimp bead and into the bead, creating an eye and hiding the final end. Close the crimp bead. Finish both ends the same way.

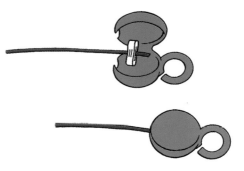

Ending with a Knot Cover

You can make various forms of knot covers. Some have a hole in them so that the wire can stick out and be fastened off with a crimp bead. Others close around the wire, which is already fastened with a crimp bead (see above).

FLOATING BRILLIANT

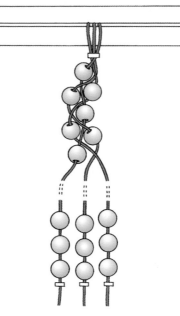

MATERIALS AND TOOLS

Brilliant-cut crystal set stone

20 inches (50 cm) of monofilament

2 crimp beads

2 rings made from 18-gauge (1 mm) sterling silver wire on a 4-mm mandrel

Sterling silver spring ring clasp, 5 mm in diameter

Photo on page 73

String the stone onto the monofilament through one side of the setting. Cut it to the desired length, allowing enough for eyes. Make an eye in each end with crimp beads. It's not necessary to put a bead on the end, as monofilament doesn't scratch the way wire does.

Finish with a ring on each end and a clasp. The stone should move freely on the string.

BRAIDING TIGER TAIL

Always braid with the finest possible wire, preferably .4 mm in gray. If you're using colored wire, .5 mm wire is fine. Wire has its own ideas and goes its own way if it's not held firmly in place when braided with beads.

Set a crimp bead over the three wire strands, about 2 inches (5 cm) in from the end. Clamp the wires in a vise while braiding them.

Your life will be easier if you string all the beads onto the wire before you start braiding. Close off each strand of wire with a crimp bead at the end.

With three strands, braid in the usual way. Every time you change the position of a wire, slide a bead into place. Hold the beads in place, both on the center strand and on the strand with the new bead.

When the braid is long enough, cut off the crimp beads at the free end.

Set a criimp bead to hold all three wires. Now you can let go and give your hands a well-deserved rest.

Finish with either a bead (page 70) or a knot cover (page 72).

BRAIDED BEAD BRACELET

 Length: 6 ½ inches (16 cm) without clasp

MATERIALS AND TOOLS

36 inches (90 cm) of tiger tail

Crimp beads

54 beads in various shades of blue, 4 mm in diameter

Sterling silver spring ring clasp, 5 mm in diameter

Photo on page 72

Cut the wire in three pieces, each 12 inches (30 cm) long. Set a crimp bead about 2 inches (5 cm) in from one end and clamp the wires in the vise.

String the beads onto the wires, about 18 beads per strand. Secure each strand with a crimp bead after the last bead is threaded on.

Braid and finish as described at left.

BRAIDED BEAD NECKLACE

 Length: 16 inches (40 cm) without clasp

MATERIALS AND TOOLS

10 feet (3 m) of tiger tail

Crimp beads

120 polymer clay or glass beads, 5 mm in diameter

2 knot covers (optional)

2 jump rings for clasp

Sterling silver clasp, 11 mm

Photos on pages 60 and 72

Cut the wire into three equal pieces, 5 ⅓ inches (13 ⅓ cm), and secure them together with a crimp bead 2 inches (5 cm) in from the end. Clamp them in the vise.

Thread 40 beads on each strand. Secure each wire end with a crimp bead when all the beads are on. Braid as previously described. End with beads or knot covers. Mount the jump rings and clasp. Be careful not to make the chain too long; it should rest fairly close to the throat.

CROCHETED CHAIN WITH PINK AND WHITE PEARLS

 Length: 15 ¼ inches (38 cm) without clasp

MATERIALS AND TOOLS

.999 silver or colored copper wire, 28 gauge (.3 mm)

40 pink and white pearls and beads in assorted shades and shapes

Size B-1 (2.5 mm) crochet hook

4 rings made from 18-gauge (1 mm) sterling silver wire on a 4-mm mandrel

Sterling silver clasp, 8 mm

Photo on page 73

Thread all the beads onto the wire before starting to crochet. Crochet a simple chain stitch, sliding a bead into the stitch every three stitches. The chain is crocheted in one piece. When it measures twice the final length, fasten off the end.

Set a ring through a stitch in the center.

Mount the clasp on the jump ring.

The wires at the other end are bound together by sewing through and around them with the tail end of the crocheted wire. Snip the ends close, then press them with flat-nose pliers. Set a row of jump rings around the sewing.

The chain can also be ended with cones (see page 64).

CROCHETED CHOKER IN PINK COPPER WIRE

 Length: 14 ¾ inches (37 cm) without clasp

MATERIALS AND TOOLS

Size B-1 (12.5 mm) crochet hook

Colored copper wire, 26 gauge (.4 mm)

Cut glass bicone beads, 4 mm in diameter

4 rings made from 18-gauge (1 mm) sterling silver wire on a 4-mm mandrel

Sterling silver spring ring clasp, 8 mm in diameter

Photo on page 73

Row 1: Chain stitch until you arrive at the desired length. Turn.

Row 2: Single crochet. Fasten off the wire and secure it by stitching around it a few times.

Measure 3 ⅓ feet (1 m) of wire for sewing on the beads. Fasten the wire by wrapping and sewing it through the end of the chain and pinch in the end.

Sew on the glass beads so that they're evenly spaced. End the wire the same way you started it.

In one end, set 4 jump rings. In the other end, mount the clasp.

The ends can also be finished with cones (see page 64).

COIL BEAD ON LEATHER CORD

MATERIALS AND TOOLS

Coil Bead

2-mm mandrel

3 ⅓ feet (1 m) of colored copper wire, 24 gauge (.5 mm)

3.5-mm mandrel

3 ⅓ feet (1 m) of silver-plated wire, 18 gauge (1 mm)

Coil End Pieces and S-Hook

2.5-mm mandrel

24 inches (60 cm) of silver-plated wire, 18 gauge (1 mm)

16 to 18 inches (40 to 45 cm) of leather cord, 2 mm in diameter

Photo on page 73

Make the coil bead, as described on page 12.

The coiled end pieces and the S-hook are described on page 57.

Mount the coiled bead on the leather cord. The ends are finished with coiled end pieces. Make an S-clasp and close the ring. To use this pattern for a bracelet, choose a lobster claw clasp instead of an S-hook.

COIL BEAD ON NECK RING

MATERIALS AND TOOLS

For the Coil Bead

Small coil: 6⅝ feet (2 m) of 24-gauge (.5 mm) colored copper wire on 2-mm mandrel

Large coil: 5 feet (1.5 m) of 18-gauge (1 mm) silver-plated wire on 3.5-mm mandrel

14 inches (35 cm) of copper wire, 8 gauge (3 mm), or a purchased reclosable silver-plated neck ring

Photo on page 73

Make the coil bead, as shown on page 12. Form the necklace around something round that's the right size. Lay the wire on a piece of leather and pound it lightly with the plastic hammer to harden the wire and make the shape more durable. Or use a purchased, closed necklace. These can be purchased in silver or gold-filled wire. Set the coil bead onto the necklace.

BRAIDED RING II

MATERIALS AND TOOLS

5⅞ feet (1.8 m) of colored copper wire, 26 or 24 gauge (.4 or .5 mm)

Photo on page 73

Cut the wire into six 12-inch (30-cm) pieces. Bend the wire in half. Secure the wires in a vise 1¼ inches (3 cm) from the end. Divide the wires, with six on each side. Group them by twos so that three pairs are on each side. Braid in the same way as for the ring on page 62.

NECK RING WITH LAVENDER BEADS

MATERIALS AND TOOLS

20 inches (50 cm) of silver-plated wire, 16 gauge (1.2 mm)
40 lavender beads, 6 mm in diameter
5 feet (1.5 m) of silver-plated wire, 26 gauge (.4 mm)
Crimp beads
4 rings made from 18-gauge (1 mm) sterling silver wire on a 4-mm mandrel
Sterling silver lobster claw clasp, 8 mm

Photo on page 72

With a pair of round-nose pliers, make an eye in one end of the 16-gauge (1.2 mm) wire, (see page 19). Cut the wire to the right length, then form an eye in the other end.

The beads are set on as shown in the drawing.

For easy work, thread the beads onto the 26-gauge (.4 mm) wire and secure the long end with a crimp bead to keep them from escaping.

Starting close to one eye, wrap the fine wire around the eye several times to secure the end. Pinch the end in closely. Place a bead next to the wrap, hold it there, and fasten it down by wrapping the wire around the heavier wire a couple of turns. As you work, place the beads so that they're offset from each other. Secure the end the same way at the other end.

Finish the ends with jump rings and a clasp.

COIL RING WITH BEAD

MATERIALS AND TOOLS

3⅓ feet (1 m) of sterling silver wire, 22 gauge (.6 mm)

2-mm mandrel

1 silver bead, 3 to 5 mm in diameter

Photo on page 73

Measure and cut 32 inches (80 cm) of the wire and make the coil. Cut the completed coil to the right length for the ring. Set the bead on the remaining piece of wire, then thread it through the coil. When the wire emerges from the coil, stick it through the bead in the opposite direction.

Tighten the wire so that the bead sits firmly in place. Wrap the coil ends around the inside wire, close to the bead. Pinch the ends closed.

PEARL AND SILVER WIRE BRACELET

 Length: 6⅞ inches (17 cm) without clasp

MATERIALS AND TOOLS

3⅞ feet (1.2 m) of 24- or 22-gauge (.5- or .6-mm) sterling silver or comparable wire

Pearls in assorted sizes and shades of gray and white

2 rings made from 18-gauge (1 mm) sterling silver wire on a 4-mm mandrel

Sterling silver lobster claw clasp, 11 mm

Photo on page 72

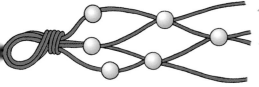

Cut the wire into four 10½-inch (27 cm) pieces. Shape one end of the bundle of wires into an eye, as shown above.

Randomly thread the pearls onto the wire. When you reach the right length, end with another eye like the first one. Set a jump ring in each eye and a clasp at one end.

CHAIN BRACELET WITH PINK BEADS

 Length: 7¼ inches (18 cm) without clasp

MATERIALS AND TOOLS

46 rings made from 16-gauge (1.2 mm) sterling silver wire on a 4-mm mandrel

15 bright pink beads, 4 to 8 mm in diameter

20 inches (50 cm) of .999 silver wire, 24 gauge (.5 mm)

Sterling silver spring ring clasp, 7 mm

Photo on page 73

Assemble, following the directions for the Anchor Chain with Beads on page 50.

RING WITH PINK PEARL

MATERIALS AND TOOLS

3¼ inches (8 cm) of sterling silver wire, 12 gauge (2 mm)

4 inches (10 cm) of .999 silver wire, 24 gauge (.5 mm), to mount the pearl

1 pink pearl, 5 mm in diameter

Photo on page 73

Shape the heavier wire around a ring mandrel (see page 17). File the ends.

Tie in the pearl as shown on page 50.

It's easy to change the bead any time, so try some different possibilities right away. This ring is also handsome plain, worn on your thumb.

COLLAR WITH BLUE CRYSTAL BEADS

 Length: 16 inches (40 cm) without clasp

MATERIALS AND TOOLS

10 feet (3 m) of tiger tail, .4 mm

Crimp beads

20 crystal set stones, 6 mm in diameter

Knot covers

30 rings made from 18-gauge (1 mm) sterling silver wire on a 4-mm mandrel

Sterling silver lobster claw clasp, 9 mm

Photo on page 72

Cut the wire into three 3⅓-foot (1 m) lengths. Secure them together with a crimp bead, 2 inches (5 cm) in from one end.

Use the drawing as a guide to assemble the necklace. There's a cross on the back of the set stones, which makes it possible to run two wires through them. Set all the crimp beads and stones in place *before* tightening the crimps. That way you'll be able to adjust the shape of the curves somewhat.

Secure the stones by pinching crimp beads on all four sides of each stone.

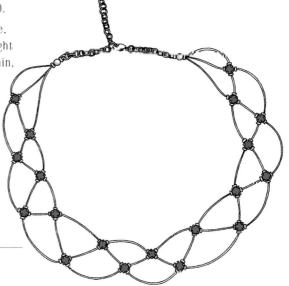

End with knot covers, a chain of rings on both ends, and a clasp.

On the next page is a drawing with an actual-size template for this project. Use it to space the stones at the proper distance from one another.

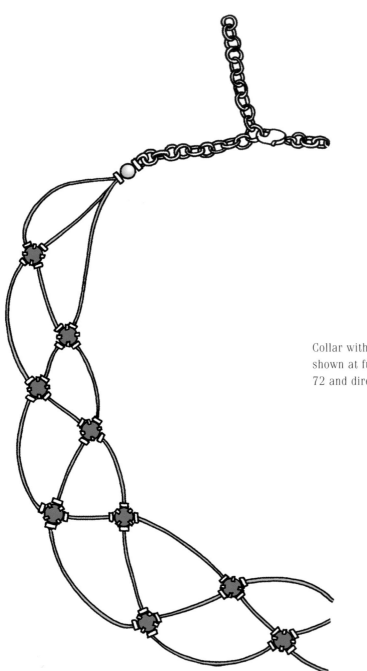

Collar with Blue Crystal Beads
shown at full size. Photo on page
72 and directions on page 77.

TOOLS AND KEY TO WIRE GAUGES

The author's original round-wire specifications were adapted to U.S. standards using Brown & Sharpe (or American) wire gauge (AWG) specifications and their equivalent *rounded* metric measurements. Intermediate (i.e., odd-numbered) wire sizes were converted to those that are readily available in the U.S. Refer to the chart below to find the U.K. equivalent using Imperial (or British Standard) Wire Gauge (SWG) specifications.

Sterling Silver Gauge	AWG Diameter	SWG Diameter
28	.3 mm	.4 mm
26	.4 mm	.5 mm
24	.5 mm	.6 mm
22	.6 mm	.7 mm
20	.8 mm	.9 mm
18	1.0 mm	1.2 mm
16	1.2 mm	1.6 mm
14	1.5 mm	2.0 mm
12	2.0 mm	2.1 mm

1. Colored copper wire
2. Eggbeater hand drill
3. Coiling tool
4. Rotary tumbler
5. Hardwood drawing block with holes
6. Steel shot
7. Plastic hammer
8. Crochet hook
9. Knitting needles
10. Wide flat-nose pliers
11. Files
12. Narrow flat-nose pliers
13. Curved needle-nose pliers
14. Round-nose pliers
15. Wire cutters
16. Bracelet mandrel
17. Pasta maker
18. Wooden cone
19. Mandrels for making coils
20. Crimp beads
21. Metal bead tips
22. Silver wire
23. Hematite rings
24. Ring mandrel
25. Skewers
26. Silver rings
27. Jeweler's saw
28. Vise
29. Set stones